Looking for the Phoenix

Looking for the Phoenix
A Memoir

W. H. OLIVER

BRIDGET WILLIAMS BOOKS

First published in 2002 by Bridget Williams Books Limited, P O Box 5482, Wellington

© W. H. Oliver

This book is copyright. Apart from fair dealing for the purpose of private study, research, criticism, or review, as permitted under the Copyright Act, no part may be reproduced by any process without the prior permission of the publishers.

Publication was assisted by the College of Humanities and Social Sciences, Massey University, and the History Group, Ministry for Culture and Heritage.

ISBN 1-877242-98-5

National Library of New Zealand Cataloguing-in-Publication Data
Oliver, W. H. (William Hosking), 1925-
Looking for the phoenix : a memoir / W. H. Oliver.
ISBN 1-877242-98-5
1. Oliver, W. H. (William Hosking), 1925- 2. Historians—New Zealand—Biography. 3. Poets, New Zealand—20th century—Biography. I. Title.
993.032092—dc 21
Biography.

Cover design: Mission Hall DGL
Internal design and typesetting: Afineline/Archetype
Printed by: Astra Print

To My Families

CONTENTS

	Acknowledgements	ix
ONE	A Colonial Future	1
TWO	A Home in a Strange Land	18
THREE	Making a Better World	35
FOUR	People of the Word	52
FIVE	A Time of Opening	65
SIX	Departures and Journeys	82
SEVEN	Finding a Country	94
EIGHT	An Expanding Horizon	109
NINE	A Time of Turning	125
TEN	A Crowded Portrait Gallery	138
ELEVEN	Histories and Politics	154
TWELVE	A History to Live By	171

ACKNOWLEDGEMENTS

This book arose from two conversations, one late in 1999 and the other around the middle of 2000. The first was with a convalescent friend on a Golden Bay beach; here I found myself retelling some of my parents' stories about their early years in Cornwall and remembering some of my own from a North Island country childhood.

That friend, a publisher I had worked with on many books, suggested that these tales might grow into a larger story. Over the next three years that account of origins and inheritance expanded into an exploration of the history I had lived through – and occasionally tried to influence – and the history I have written over the last half century. The book owes much to that summer-time story-telling and more to the editorial insights and skills which helped it come to life. It was her eye, also, that caught the phrase 'looking for the phoenix', harking back to my first book.

The second conversation had a different aim. The idea of a family history was discussed at a gathering held to celebrate my sister's birthday. Though that project has not yet been fulfilled, a substantial instalment is to be found in the first three chapters of this book. My sister Peg and my brother John have read these chapters and helped me with comments and corrections. It is a great sorrow that my brother died before he had a chance to read the whole book.

My children have read all or part of an earlier draft and have contributed significantly to the final text. I warmly appreciate their interest and their comments. My friend of more than fifty years, Neil Mountier, and my colleagues, Claudia Orange and Alan Ward, have also made valuable suggestions. Other friends have offered advice and encouragement. Errors and omissions that may persist are, however, my sole responsibility.

W. H. Oliver
Wellington, 2002

CHAPTER ONE

A Colonial Future

William Henry Oliver, my father, was born in 1890 and emigrated from Cornwall to New Zealand in his twentieth year. Four years later he sailed away to the Great War – to Egypt, the Dardanelles, England and France and eventually to Cornwall, where he married Ethel Amelia Hosking in 1917. They sailed back to New Zealand in 1919, and settled near Feilding. Margaret Edith was born in 1920, John George Hosking in 1922 and William Hosking in 1925. My mother's mother, Edith Hosking, joined the family before the birth of my brother and remained with it until the mid 1930s. This is the family I grew up in, living in a modest villa-type house which had grown outwards from an original cottage in a small rural settlement on Makino Road, two miles north of Feilding, clustered around the dairy factory and the railway siding.

My memories are of a man with a fine bald dome, brown as a nut and gleaming in the summer sun, but in his youth my father had had a good head of black hair, unusually for a man with clear china-blue eyes. That he was once almost bushy I knew from a photograph that used to hang in the Makino Road house, together with one of my mother as a young woman. But that photograph, a formal studio portrait taken either in Cornwall or in his early New Zealand years, has disappeared. Its testimony has become a matter of personal memory – or maybe even less than that, for no one else seems to remember it.

Photographs taken in the war years show his closely cropped hair already thinning over the temples. In one he stands beside his new wife, her broad-brimmed straw echoing his uniform 'lemon-squeezer', the emblem of the New Zealand soldier. These pictures show a sturdy figure of a man, confident and purposeful, with a powerful beak of a nose and steady eyes looking straight ahead. But they do not reveal the bent back, almost that of a hunchback, the result of a childhood illness which kept him in a sagging bed for a year. Much later a young doctor took an interest in his medical history and conjectured that in childhood, with only family care, my father had survived Pott's disease.

Memory takes many forms. Some of what we remember may come from our own and others' observation, some from more impersonal sources. But this distinction is not a sharp one and, when it is a matter of the life of a known and loved person, not a real one. For the mind is an active agent; the artefact it composes is woven from a random assemblage of recollections, echoes of recollections, guesses transformed into recollections, imagined happenings imperceptibly made real, scraps of written and printed paper, faded and discoloured photographs, newspaper clippings and materials preserved in libraries and archival collections. All these contribute to the tales I now tell about my father. Two forces, especially, shape the image I have built; first, the light still shining in my mind from that vividly remembered man and, second, my own capacity (as well as his) for invention and reinvention. Did he embroider the tales he told? He was, after all, a writer of verses, an orator, a preacher and a man of imagination. Did I invent the photograph upon which I have relied? Did I build him up in my child's mind into a larger-than-life figure? Do I do so now? Did the newspaper reporter get it right? Did the clerk in the army office make a mistake? Perhaps, perhaps not; the kinds of truth contained in memories are varied and various, but they are all truths of a kind.

The photographs of the colonial soldier were taken in convalescent hospitals and training camps and in Truro, where he was sent in 1916 to recover from an illness caused, in his opinion, by eating German sausage.

But he had been seriously ill long before that, both at Gallipoli and in France. In Truro, in 1917, he married my mother, a shop assistant who turned twenty-four in that year, the daughter of a miner who had died – presumably of miner's phthisis – eight years earlier, and of a widowed mother who ran a small shop. Truro was only a few miles from the village in which my father had been born, Fraddon, and the one nearby where he had lived for much of his childhood, the picturesquely named Indian Queens. (The legend – but only the legend – tells that Pocahontas stopped there on her way north to London in the early seventeenth century, brought to England from Virginia by John Smith.) My mother used to say that if my father had been one of the farm lads she had seen driving carts to the market in Truro ('country janners', in her phrase), she would never have looked at him. But by the time she and other young women began to visit the convalescing soldiers in the Royal Cornwall Infirmary, he had been transformed by four years in a colony and by almost as many in a colonial army into a man of some consequence and presence, a non-commissioned officer in the 1st NZEF. Her friends teased her for taking up with 'the New Zealander', not for looking at a 'country janner'.

My father had three sisters: Alma, who was the first to emigrate to New Zealand with her husband Will Stevens; Evelyn, of whom I know nothing except that she married a man called Howard Bunt; and Maggie, the one I met when I first went to Cornwall (she was then married to the same Howard, Evelyn having died some time earlier). It was a small family, compared with the eleven of which his father was the eldest, a family he looked back to with great fondness in his later years. An account of his family life is preserved in notes he made for a talk when he was in his seventies, recollecting the return journey he had made to Cornwall over ten years earlier; it is thus a memory of a memory of a distant time. Distance almost certainly lent enchantment to the remembered scene; the stories I recall him telling as a younger man about his childhood have a harsher tone.

When he revisited his family home, the cottage at Kestle Mill at the junction of three streams, he remembered the sound of birds singing in the trees in the morning. He called at the cottage but 'the lady' did not ask him to come in; I recollect from my own visit that it had been gentrified.

He found that some of the old landmarks were still there – the blacksmith's shop and the cobbler's shop. Though only three stone cottages were left, the village was still lovely with apple trees, currants, wild plums and cherries. Geese, donkeys, ponies and cows were still pastured on the common land.

The cottage in which he had been born was there when he went back sixty years later. Then he measured it carefully – it was 20 feet by 12. When he was a child it had a thatched roof, an earth floor, a turf wall and an elm tree at the back. There was one room down and two upstairs. Downstairs was the general purpose living room with a table, a stove built into the wall of the fireplace, a glass cupboard, six chairs and a little table for the Bible and *Pilgrim's Progress*. His father, John, could neither read nor write but his mother, Annie (born Trebilcock), regularly read to her family from the Bible. This home, he wrote, was built upon the Bible; faith and love were its keynotes. I remember him talking of the 'clome oben', simply a cavity in the fireplace wall with an iron door. He recalled his mother baking cakes; after a time she took out the cake and always said 'craw or daw?' – black as a crow or as white as dough? It was never either.

It was a Methodist family, adhering to the more traditional Wesleyan connection – the emotionalism of the Bible Christians and the simplicity of the Primitive Methodists were not part of his inheritance. Cornwall was predominantly Methodist; the great revival begun by John Wesley in the eighteenth century had turned well over half of the Cornish into Methodists of one sort or another. The Church of England (to which my mother's family belonged) made up only a little more than a quarter of the population. Anglicanism, some have argued, had never taken root there after the suppression of the revolt in 1549 against the introduction of the new-fangled English prayer-book to replace the immemorially familiar Latin mass, so that the people responded quickly to the warmer and more enthusiastic kind of religion brought by John Wesley.

Methodism, it is said, civilised the lawless and tumultuous Cornish, turning what had been called 'West Barbary' into 'the Delectable Duchy' – a phrase my mother fondly used. Revivals punctuated the nineteenth century; as a child I heard about the huge gatherings at Gwennap Pit, an outdoor amphitheatre, where the Cornish evangelist, Billy Bray, preached to thousands. But Methodism in Cornwall was a good deal more than revivalistic. It fostered a drive for self-help and self-improvement, a concern for the needy and a contempt of riches. It was strongly egalitarian and liberal and radical in politics; many of its adherents saw political action as a natural extension of their religious beliefs.

All these characteristics were present to a marked degree in my father; he hated privilege, did not have any respect for wealth, worked to improve the lot of the poor, and spent most of his adult life active in the Labour Party. He was strong for self-development, an autodidact and a considerable reader with a liking for history. This drive for improvement surely arose from his upbringing, from the family Bible readings and the sermons heard in chapel. From time to time he used to grumble about the burden of chapel attendance – twice on a Sunday with Sunday school in between. But he became a Methodist local preacher later in life and remained faithful to his religious inheritance through the political activity he believed to be practical Christianity.

In that Bible-reading home his literate and religious mother was undoubtedly the dominant figure. Clearly, too, she was the domestic manager (as my mother would be in her turn). She had 14s a week to manage on; she spent it on butter, cream, beef, coal, flour, barley, cocoa and lollies – a surprisingly ample list. As well, the dog caught rabbits for the table. Killing and butchering the pig was a major annual event. His father and another man would arrive and a couple of old men from the village would be recruited. They would rope the pig and a couple of 'hairy dogs' would help them pull and push the pig into position. Meanwhile he and his mother would be getting the boilers ready, four of them borrowed from neighbours. The helpers each took a piece of pork back with them. The process was repeated when the neighbours killed their pigs. In the stories he told when I was a child, 'butcher's meat' was a rarity and for the most part they lived on offal or a slice of fatty bacon from the family pig. As well, there was the traditional pasty for the midday 'crowst' eaten in the fields or the clay-pits, with a corner saved for the afternoon. It was a splendid dish if made with meat but more likely to be of leek or turnip and potatoes.

He attended school until he was twelve but schooling was often interrupted by the demands of farm work. At the age of ten he began to work for the farmer who employed his father. His wages were 8*d* rising to 1*s* a day by the time he became too big for a boy's job at fifteen; he was allowed to keep 1*s* a month. Then he had to find work on other farms and later went to the clay-pits. This is how he wrote down his story late in life; earlier, he had given it a more dramatic shape. He talked of being hired annually at Somercourt fair with his father, an employment practice that reaches back into rural antiquity and (in his mind) to class oppression and exploitation. His father he described as a meek and obedient man, for whom the life of a labourer was part of the ordained nature of things; he was horrified when one year his son proposed to ask for an increase in wages. My grandfather predicted, direfully, that my father would not be hired again, and he was not. That was, so this story goes, when he went off to work in the clay-pits.

The shift of occupation was typically Cornish. The county had three major industries – mining, farming and fishing – and I find it satisfying that my forebears were engaged in all three. The great 'staple' and the heart of the economy had been copper and tin mining, in terminal decline by the end of the nineteenth century. But by that time clay quarrying, extracting china clay for the Staffordshire potteries, had become a major activity. My father did not have to leave home to become an industrial worker; in Cornwall farming and mining went on side by side in small compact communities of clustered villages. For all its importance, my father did not regard clay mining favourably. It was hard underground work standing in water – in his opinion the only employment lower in status than that of the farm labourer. But it paid better wages, and he was already saving for emigration. For by this time, as he put it, 'my mind was overseas'; at the age of nineteen he left for New Zealand.

The minds of thousands of Cornish people had turned overseas as mining declined. Long before my father's departure, Cornwall had generated an 'emigration culture' and a brisk 'emigration trade' of agents and organisers. It has been estimated that nearly a quarter of a million Cornish people left the county in the nineteenth century, most of them for overseas.

In this 'Great Migration', extending from the 1830s to the Great War, the Cornish took their skills, especially in mining but also in farming and fishing, to North America, Australia and South Africa as well as to lesser destinations in Europe, South America and New Zealand. Some Cornish people, skilled in hard-rock mining, had been brought out by the Canterbury province to put through the Lyttelton tunnel, and a small Cornish community was established in south Canterbury.

Wherever they went, the Cornish took their sense of a distinctive identity with them. They formed clubs, founded newspapers, went in for Cornish wrestling and dancing, and evolved a nostalgic and romantic Cornishness. But my father, quite deliberately I suspect, was untouched by this sentimentality. He had, we might say, reconstructed himself as a new man in a free country. He gave up the dialect (except for humorous purposes) and took no interest in cultural Cornishness; his friends and associates were those he found around him who shared his life and his hopes. He even changed his name – or was it changed for him? In Cornwall he was always 'Harry' or the abbreviated '(H)aar' – with a hint of an aspirate and a long throaty vowel. He was still that to relatives who sent letters from home, but to all and sundry in New Zealand he became 'Bill'. (Except for my mother, who called him 'Father', while he in turn called her 'Mother'.)

However, he did retain strong memories of the places and the people he had come from. He told stories about his country childhood, sometimes for their own sake but more often to underline the beneficial difference between then and now. He survived into adulthood but only after a long childhood illness; he was certainly not the only male child born but he was the only one to live past infancy. Do I recall him saying that the same name was given to successive children, so that it would not die out? Perhaps, for that was a nineteenth century practice. The names John and William were given to successive generations of sons, their order reversed from one to the next. His grandfather was William and his father John; his father's younger brother William had died aged fourteen. (The habit persisted in the new land; my elder brother is John and I am William; his only son is William; my eldest is John and a younger is William, though he prefers his second name, Hugh.)

Some of his stories were pleasantly bucolic – bird-nesting in the long twilights, taking only one warm egg from the nests in the quickset hedges (his father was a skilled hedger) and blowing it empty through holes at each end. And making whistles from green elder twigs by easing the bark from the slippery wood and sliding it up and down to modulate the sound – decades later he noticed an elder in our Palmerston North garden and made a whistle on the spot with his pocket knife. These tales suggest, like his late life recollections, that his childhood was not quite as bleak as other stories suggest.

After his second return to Cornwall, he talked and wrote glowingly of the warmth and beauty of his home and of the great improvements his surviving childhood friends and relations now enjoyed, thanks (as he firmly believed) to the Labour government returned to office in Britain in 1945. He may have seen in this the home country catching up with the colony, which had had the good sense to elect such a government ten years earlier and, of course, had been a better place all along. This is an irony that he probably could not have let himself appreciate: after the four decades between his departure and his return, he and his contemporaries who had stayed behind had ended up in much the same condition of modest well-being. Perhaps history has a hard way with the impatient ones. He was certainly impatient, and despite the irony I can find in myself nothing but respect and praise for his refusal to be patient – and gratitude, for I doubt if my own contemporaries raised in Cornwall could have counted on the opportunities or the luck I took, I think rightly, for granted.

Two of the stories he told in his younger years, always with undiminished indignation, exemplify the harshness of the life he was intent upon leaving behind. The first was of working in the fields in the bitter winter cold pulling turnips and cutting off their tops with raw bare hands. I could almost see and hear the child crying with pain as he worked. These were the farm tasks for which he was regularly taken away from school, so that he grew up incompletely literate, probably more able (it was a common pattern) to read than to write. The second is a curious tale – of being required by the farmer to milk a mare after foaling, perhaps because the foal had been stillborn or had died. He must have been quite small, for the task had terrified him and he considered it to be inexplicably inhuman of his employer. I still find it a bizarre and indeed a frightening image.

The social structure of nineteenth century rural Cornwall was characterised by the familiar three-tier system of landlord, tenant farmer and labourer but, compared with England as a whole, the gentry were thin on the ground and less dominant. Small-scale farming by tenant farmers and smallholders predominated. This, it has been said, fostered a lack of class consciousness and a spirit of egalitarianism. But these generalisations may be less than apt for those below the tenant farmers – the labourers and the wage workers. Certainly my father did not think he had grown up in an egalitarian society. The rural hierarchy of his childhood consisted of the squire who was an army colonel ('we were scared of him'), the farmer who was 'addressed as Sir' and his wife as 'Mam', and the farm labourer who was treated as an equal. Late in life he saw more harmony in this order than he had earlier, and thought that all three classes had had a part in building what he believed to be the greatness of Britain and her empire. But even in that mellow mood he asserted with some vehemence the claim of the peasant to an eminent place in the British story, especially in the settlement of the colonies overseas. In his earlier stories he had taken a less tolerant view of social hierarchy; then the villain was the tenant farmer. He brought that animosity to New Zealand and shared the anti-farmer feeling of the early Labour Party.

From his early years he grew plants and vegetables for sale and saved the proceeds, tiny sums which grew slowly, perhaps in a savings account. Money from his wages as a farm labourer and a worker in the clay-pits would have gone there too, though most went to meet his share of family costs. Bit by bit, he had put together enough for a passage, £19, by 1910. He said that when he reached Plymouth it was the first time he had seen the sea, although he lived no more than a few miles from Newquay on the northern coast. I grew up with the idea of a young man tramping from central Cornwall to distant Plymouth with his few pounds in his pocket and Canada as his intended destination, boarding a ship for New Zealand just because it was there. I had persuaded myself that all this happened in 1906, when he was a mere sixteen and setting out, heroically, on his own.

It was not so; he left at nineteen with others from his village, Ned Osborne and Moyse Hocking and their wives. They had surely planned to go to Timaru where his sister, Alma, and her husband Will Stevens already lived. It is likely that their emigration had been managed by one of the many agents in the 'emigration trade'. I am sorry for the loss of the more heroic story, wrought perhaps by his own telling, certainly by my imagination. He did say, I am sure, that after his first meal on the ship he felt satisfied for the first time in his life.

He arrived in New Zealand in 1910 and enlisted in the army in Feilding in 1914. In between there is a gap which I can fill only with a few imprecise but meaningful details. He does not seem to have stayed long in Timaru; he told of delivering milk to households in Sumner, Christchurch, and of working with a harvesting gang on the Canterbury wheat farms. He spoke, too, of living in a boarding house for working men somewhere around the Christchurch railway station. Young single men on the move in search of work were common at that time and numerous boarding houses catered for them. No doubt he enjoyed the plentiful plain fare, for food always figured prominently in his reminiscences. In his maturity I remember him as a rapid and prodigious eater. His liking for both butter and cream (Cornish clotted cream) with bread and jam earned my more abstemious and frugal mother's disapproval.

So I feel sure that he ate heartily wherever he was in these hidden years and that the staple colonial diet – mutton, potatoes and vegetables, puddings and bread and butter – was a constant pleasure. That was certainly the case on the job with the harvesting gang, working with a threshing machine driven by a stationary steam engine. Chiefly he remembered the quantities of white bread liberally spread with golden syrup, the celebrated colonial 'cocky's joy'. He would eat neither brown bread, perhaps out of a revulsion from the black bread of his childhood, nor beetroot, because it reminded him of red mangolds, food for cattle.

This was the kind of work he had been brought up to do, and he did it well. Pitchfork, long-handled shovel, scythe and sickle – these were the tools he was born to use. He was an artist with the shovel, trenching the sod for a vegetable garden or, when working on the roads, spreading gravel in a wide even arc. Once at Makino Road he decided to dig a well; we were outside the town supply and dependent on tanks of rain water. These would be anxiously tapped each summer to measure the dwindling contents. If the dry weather lasted (as, in my recollection, it always did), water would have to be carted from the dairy factory in the back of the Model T in kerosene tin buckets. A dowser, equipped with his bendy willow twig, was employed; the wand dipped down, pointing to underground water. I remember my father at the bottom of a narrow pit something like twice his height, his bald head glistening with sweat, throwing with unfailing accuracy shovelfuls of clay to the surface. The well was a work of art, the walls absolutely smooth and straight. But there was no water. That, in retrospect, seems a suitable symbol for the depression years in which it was dug.

At some point in these hidden years my father went to the North Island and settled in Feilding. This was in a time when men were moving from the South to the North Island in search of work. The Department of Labour sent them to places where jobs were available by providing a single rail fare, which they were required to pay back and, generally speaking, did. Perhaps my father was among those beneficiaries of the innovations of William Pember Reeves and Edward Tregear in the 1890s, reformers whose achievements I would later set graduate students to study. Whether assisted or not, he was part of the movement of labouring men from the static south to the expanding rural economy of the north. Feilding, where he put down his roots, was a small and busy town in the heart of a flourishing dairying district.

He may have worked on farms for a start, but by the time he emerges into the record (when he enlisted in August 1914), he was living in a boarding house and working for the Feilding Sash and Door Co Ltd. He gave his occupation on enlistment as 'Timber Classer'. He could not have learned this skill in Cornwall and probably not on the Canterbury plains; it is most likely that he had acquired his new trade in Feilding. He loved working with sawn timber in the mill yards, stacking the long planks for delivery to customers. He had, for an unschooled man, an uncanny capacity to convert 'running feet' into 'super feet' – that is, planks of various dimensions into a standard measure for charging out. He claimed to be able to do it in his head, with the stub of a carpenter's pencil and a slab of wood. Fittingly his last job (after the Second World War) was that of a yardman with a small timber mill in Dannevirke. In between there was much else, by way of employment and unemployment, but nothing that he liked more. Long after he ceased work at the Sash and Door, he gave his occupation as 'timber salesman' or 'salesman' in the electoral rolls.

In Feilding, to speculate only a little, he completed the metamorphosis from emigrant to New Zealander. Perhaps the studio portrait with the abundant head of hair was taken around this time – it has (or had) the look of a settled, confident young man. His life probably now took on a more stable pattern. Almost certainly he went to school in Feilding and gained his Proficiency, the top leaving qualification from primary school. In 1913 the Feilding Technical School was offering 'Students who are deficient in general education' the opportunity to enrol in 'continuation classes for preparation for a Standard VI certificate'. The Proficiency certificate was still around many years later, when children used to sit on the grass and count up the chevron-like seeds on rye grass stems to forecast their fate: 'Pro, Comp, Fail'. This was a serious business; Proficiency allowed you to go on to secondary school; Competency was the route to trade and commercial employment; Failure meant the outer darkness of unskilled labour. But he would have been too old for secondary school, and in any case the war intervened. My father's future, in spite of this qualification, was in semi-skilled and unskilled labour. He returned to formal education in the 1920s and 1930s, through the Workers Educational Association.

Both the Oddfellows (Manchester Unity) Friendly Society and the United Labour Party were active in Feilding in those pre-war years. Membership of the Oddfellows would have come easily to a young man reared in the virtues of self-help and, in his early twenties, almost certainly looking forward to marriage and family. It seems reasonable to suppose that he joined these organisations around this time; he was certainly active in both after his return from the war. There can, too, be little doubt that he attended the Methodist church; at his enlistment he gave his religion as Wesleyan.

It is almost certain, too, that in Feilding he 'improved' himself by going to an elocutionist and learning to talk without an accent, a distinctly 'naturalising' strategy in a time when immigrants often remained identifiable by their accents. From as far back as I can recall, he had two voices, 'proper' (but not 'posh') English and Cornish English. The latter we heard only when a few 'Cousin Jacks' were gathered together and laughed uproariously (but not derisively) at jokes cracked in the old tongue. The accent was, I think, something he treasured as a memory and deliberately outgrew. My mother always sniffed at these displays; she recognised the dialect but her speech had been formed by proper schools in Truro. But perhaps she had had both; much later I stayed with her Land's End farming relatives and found that the school-age daughter had the same two voices – 'proper' for school and Cornish for home.

I remember the Feilding drill hall as a large low wooden building with a corrugated iron roof. Here, in my childhood, church 'bring and buys' and school concerts were held; I can recall, from my very early years, standing petrified on the stage and gabbling out a patriotic poem beginning 'What can a little chap do / For his country and for you?' It went on to state that he could fight for the right with all of his might. That hall is where my father would have gone to enlist on 15 August 1914, on the very outbreak of war, to join the West Coast Company of the Wellington Infantry Battalion. He claimed to have been the second to enlist in Feilding; his mate was the first and was killed. He was certainly intent upon fighting for the right but he was not a little chap – army records show that he was quite sturdy at 12 stone and 5 foot 9 inches. He was barrel-chested (chest expansion 36½–40½ inches) with blue eyes and brown – family tradition says black – hair, good teeth, normal sight and hearing, and good physical condition. He had already served in the Territorials, having registered for compulsory military service under the 1909 Act. He named his mother as next of kin.

He went to the army camp at the Awapuni racecourse in Palmerston North; perhaps he was among those enthusiastically farewelled from the Feilding railway station, a few days after his enlistment, to begin their life as soldiers in wet and muddy conditions. Training went on for the next two months, until his company embarked on the *Maunganui* in Wellington. The fleet of transports and escorts left Wellington on the morning of 16 October 1914 with the Main Body of the 1st NZEF for further training in Egypt. The ships called at Hobart, Albany (in Western Australia), Colombo and Aden, and passed through the Suez Canal, to disembark the force at Alexandria early in December. So he returned to the old world as a young man remade by the new – but still a new world unable to avoid a part in the disasters and triumphs of the old.

In Egypt he learned a few phrases of Arabic; 'imshi alla' (so, at least, he pronounced it) is the only one I can remember. It meant 'get out of the way' and I now wonder, shamefacedly, if the white supremacist in him enjoyed ordering beggars and 'lesser breeds' out of his path. However, a socialist in the making, he thought more keenly of the multitudes of slaves who had laboured and died to build the pyramids than of their antiquity. A common response, and one which demonstrates his self-identification with the toiling and suffering masses throughout history.

Like many returned soldiers, he spoke little of the war and not at all about the actual fighting. He suffered from recurrent nightmares for as long as I can remember. He attributed them to a later experience of being chased, within an inch of his life, by a bull while travelling on a country road. I suspect that some experience at Gallipoli or on the Western Front was the real cause. Once, having found a copy of F. Waite's *The New Zealanders at Gallipoli* in a library, I showed him an illustration of the laden barges landing on the beaches. He became excited and exclaimed 'I was there! I was there!' But not another word.

He embarked for the Dardanelles from Alexandria on 12 April 1915 and spent over three months at Gallipoli before being invalided to the hospital at Mudros on Lemnos; it was the island's peace rather than its beauty that stayed in his mind. Early in October he rejoined his battalion for another month; falling ill again, he was hospitalised, and soon taken to England on the *Lusitania*. (After the evacuation of the Dardanelles, the New Zealand troops were sent to England, including some 2,000 who were convalescent.) In mid December he was admitted to a hospital in Birmingham, after a time in camp at Epsom. Apart from the spell in

Lemnos, I know nothing of this from his own account, but only from his army records. He had made his contribution to Gallipoli; he shared in the subsequent legend as a returned soldier through RSA membership and Anzac Day parades rather than through the birth-of-a-nation talk which became common later. At the time, I feel sure, he was wholly concerned with the dreadfulness of fighting and the effects of illnesses variously identified as enterocolitis, enteritis and paratyphoid.

Two peaceful years in England followed. He spent the first half of 1916 in hospital and in the training depot at Hornchurch. In July he was taken on strength again at the Command Depot at Codford and at the training depot at Sling camp, both on the Salisbury Plain. He qualified at Aldershot as an instructor in physical drill and bayoneting (the idea that such a gentle man had become expert at that form of fighting is hard to take in) and was promoted lance-corporal. By the end of 1916 he was at the Royal Cornwall Infirmary in Truro, where he met my mother. He must have courted her at a distance, with spells of leave back in Cornwall, for he was in Codford again as an instructor early in 1917. In September he was promoted temporary sergeant, in time to enable him to wear his three stripes for his wedding.

Their married life had to wait until the war, and his part in it, was over – the best part of another two years. In April 1918, by now a full sergeant, he left Codford for France, and in June 'marched out' from Etaples to join his battalion in the field. There he survived the last German offensive in 1918 which ended with the armistice in November. For a brief time the New Zealand Division was part of the occupying force stationed in Cologne. A long panorama photograph of Cologne hanging on the wall at Makino Road has long since disappeared, but I recall the many bridges across a very blue Rhine.

Of the horrors of war on the Western Front, as of those at the Dardanelles, he spoke hardly a word – only of having his hat shot through when he put it on the top of the trench. He was never wounded and lucky not to have been; in the 1930s it was discovered after an operation, almost too late, that he was a haemophiliac. On 17 March 1919 he and his wife Ethel embarked on the *Remuera* from Plymouth; there were separate quarters for the soldiers and for their wives. They arrived in Auckland on his birthday, 5 May, when his foreign service of (as he said with pride) 4 years and 202 days came at last to an end. He went through the entire war, including long spells at two of its fiercest theatres, without a scratch, at least to body; the wounds of the spirit were another matter, but always remained concealed.

From Auckland they took the overnight train to Feilding, and quite soon bought the house they were to live in for nearly twenty years. My father reckoned that he had been done out of £100 from his gratuity by the lawyer acting for the seller. Whatever the truth of the matter, he believed that he, a returned soldier, had been swindled by a man who was a pillar of his own Methodist church. But that house is part of my mother's story, of a home made in a land that never quite became familiar. In that home his life was that of the breadwinner, the husbandman and the labourer; outside but dependent upon it, he began the career of radical politician in the conservative rural heartland.

But his wartime story does not really end for another half-century. In 1965, he went with a group of Australians and New Zealanders to the fiftieth anniversary celebrations at Gallipoli. After the long flight to Cairo, the old men (he was seventy-five at the time and many were older) were taken around the Mediterranean and to the Dardanelles on a Greek ship. The old places, as well as some new ones in Italy and Greece, were revisited and the ceremonies observed. But he hated the oily Greek food and began the long flight home quite unwell. He was in physical distress on the plane and completed the journey, to the alarm of the cabin crew, curled up on the floor. He never quite recovered and died of a stroke two years later. Gallipoli, you might say, had got him in the end.

I received the news in the comfort of an Oxford college, spending my days in the Bodleian, on research that had at its centre the pioneer socialist and self-made man, Robert Owen. Fitting, in a way – my father knew a good deal about Owen and the co-operative movement. And, more, without his determination to find a better life, I would never have known that there was such an historical problem nor found the means to work on it. His chosen epitaph was 'Asleep in the dreamless dust', from a favourite writer, the American Ralph Ingersoll. But he has instead a simple returned serviceman's plaque. Earlier, in the notes he made for a talk, he had set down a few lines which would serve as a better memorial:

> Now I cannot visualise anything better.
> Than to live in this lovely land in peace and plenty.
> A very modest home a wife children and grandchildren.
> To grow old comes to all of us
> But keep busy and enjoy life to the full.
> Never be out of something to do.
> I can look back over a life of 73 years without any regrets and can truthfully say God has been good.

CHAPTER TWO

A Home in a Strange Land

My father proposed to my mother at a spot known as Sunny Corner, by the River Fal in Truro. He was, with all the headstrong passion that characterised his life, deeply in love. My mother, and here I must conjecture because she was a reserved person, must have been so too, for she was accepting a husband who was, in terms of social class and family expectations, not of her level. Her own mother, my formidable grandmother, was vehemently opposed to the match and expressed herself to that effect. She had, it is still remembered, fancied my mother's chances with a well-to-do farming cousin. But the ceremony went ahead; there survives a little card printed in gold letters with 'Ethel Hosking' at top left with an arrow through it and going on to read 'With Sergt. & Mrs. W. H. Oliver's Compliments'. It gives my mother's address, '24 Richmond Hill, Truro' and the date of the wedding, 'October 8th, 1917'.

Years later I chanced upon an old notebook of my father's and read out, as something of a joke (for which now only shame can be felt), his heartfelt declaration: 'My God is humanity, my hope my darling wife.' He was embarrassed and angry. For all the difficulties that lay ahead, and for all his outside preoccupations and the time he spent away from home, I do not think that he ever repudiated this avowal. My parents were unalike in both style and temperament but through their differences they complemented each other. In every photograph taken in their early married years, she is reserved and inward-looking, he faces the world with a steady and challenging gaze. It would be easy to depict her as living in the shadow of this vigorous man – easy, but wide of the mark. Her strength was exercised in the domestic arena but it was by no means less than his; on her chosen ground it was the greater. And if his personality was more vivid and outgoing, hers was no less clear and emphatic.

The photograph of my mother which hung on the wall of the Makino Road house was enlarged from a group photograph of (probably) the shop girls employed by Gill's, a Truro establishment I now know to call N. Gill & Son, Drapers. Gill's in 1912, by which time she would have been working there, advertised 'Ready to wear dresses from 2/11 each to 4 Guineas', as well as 'Household linens. Replenish your stock at sale prices.' She talked of selling those many small items known as haberdashery, of hurrying to place a chair for an important customer while a more senior assistant attended to her wants, of 'old Mr Gill' pacing through the shop and silently leaving a long fingermark on any dusty surface. She was not, I seem to recall, paid anything during a probationary period, before she became the 'Draper's Assistant' specified in her marriage lines. She seemed to accept that situation with an equanimity my father might well not have felt. He, however, might have reasoned that it did not matter so much because work for young women was an interim between the parental and the marital home.

The picture shows a serious young woman with a longish face and nose, heavy brows, short thick hair parted on the left, smooth cheeks, and a firm mouth and chin. She was, in a reticent way, very beautiful; this beauty illuminates a series of photographs going back to her infancy and forward into her years as a married woman. I can readily believe that in 1917 my convalescing father, with the awfulness of the Dardanelles and his long illness behind him, was utterly entranced and swept off his country janner's feet. Though the image shows only the head and shoulders, there is a hint of the compact stoutness she developed in later life, and more than a hint of the firm sense of what was proper and what was not that she exhibited as a wife and a mother.

Her father, George Glasson Hosking, was one of the poorer members of that large clan variously named in family records and on gravestones in rural churchyards as Hoskin, Hosken and Hosking, most of whom lived in the Land's End district. The better-off were tenant farmers, some holding land from Lord St Levan, whose seat was at St Michael's Mount. While many of the family were less than well-to-do, all that I have ever heard of or met were distinctly respectable. Cornish people are commonly known as Cousin Jacks; it has been suggested that this is because they are pretty well all related to each other. In this instance, the cousinage had been multiplied by marriages with the Williams, Jackson and Hutchings families. So numerous are the connections that the colonial offshoot visiting those parts finds it hard not to believe that he is related to the entire population – and descended from the former population, for he will find a multitude of family names in the churchyards.

George Glasson Hosking was born in 1862 into a family of three; his father had died while he was an infant, and he was raised by a bachelor uncle, Samson Hoskin, known as 'Cap'n Sam'. A captain of the mining not the marine kind (probably the agent of the mine owner and responsible for measuring the output of the individual miners), Cap'n Sam lived in the mill house at Lamorna Cove, one of the loveliest places on the south Cornwall coast. A legendary figure in my childhood, the epitome, the acme, of miserliness, he died at a great age in 1910; the verse on his black-edged funeral card reads 'Good was his heart, and in friendship sound / Patient in pain and loved by all around.' But the family legend has it otherwise. He would, it was recounted, offer my grandfather a halfpenny to go without his breakfast and then demand it back before he would give him his tea. No wonder my grandfather left for overseas (perhaps like my father he wanted to eat better). In all probability, like his stingy uncle before him, he worked in the mines of western Cornwall before taking off for North America and the Colorado mines, sometime before 1890.

My grandmother, according to the family story, had gone to Colorado after a family quarrel to live with a brother in Russell Gulch; Elizabeth and Frederick Westcott were witnesses there to the marriage of Edith Westcott and George Glasson Hosking in 1890. The certificate is a flamboyant affair, festooned with angels and cherubs, and bearing the likenesses of my grandparents. He has a soft face, with a weak chin and a faint moustache; she is sitting boldly upright, with the slightly bulging eyes I remember so well from my childhood. My mother's older sister, Jane, was born there in the following year; by 1893, when my mother was born, they were back in Cornwall living in the parish of Stithians, some distance west of Truro. Perhaps characteristically, I had managed to preserve a different story: that my grandmother had pursued him to Colorado to 'save' him from the attentions of the loose women frequenting the mining districts.

And, in fact, my grandfather did wander; he was one of the many Cornishmen who spent their working lives overseas and sent remittances home. He and his family were poor on their return to Cornwall and there is no record of how he earned his living while the further two children, Will and George (also a wandering man who spent most of his working life on ships), were born in 1895 and 1897. At some point, after his return from Colorado, he went to South Africa; perhaps he came home from time to time before the family was completed.

He spent time on the goldfields of the Rand and on the diamond fields of Kimberley, supervising African labour. I remember vividly a group photograph of the 'Witwatersrand Cornish Association' on the wall at Makino Road, twenty or so men in their working clothes, one of them, incongruously enough, black. But the tattered and browning image I have disinterred has no such legend and shows six Africans squatting in the front row, a clerkish person in a boater and a tie, and the rest of the men in working clothes and caps, a number of them smoking pipes. My grandfather sits rather glumly in the second row, by this time with a heavy moustache. Amongst the few momentoes of the African years is a small card my mother kept; it shows children dancing around a Christmas tree, and is inscribed 'To Ethel from Papa'. He returned to Truro in time to die, at the age of forty-six, in 1909.

In the following year Cap'n Sam died and, so the story goes, my grandmother was bitterly disappointed to find that he left her family no legacy. The well-to-do Hoskings excited both the envy and the hopes of their poorer relations. Edith, according to an account not wholly inconsistent with the other stories, had originally pursued George Glasson to Colorado to secure the legacy supposed to be due to him from the ageing captain. Hopes of advantage from other 'rich' Hoskings travelled to New Zealand and were still quite lively in my childhood.

My grandmother brought up her family – they ranged in years from eighteen to twelve when her husband died – by keeping a small shop; she sold, among much else, home-made ice cream. My mother's childhood was not an affluent one; everyone worked hard and her mother watched every penny, because she needed to. But it was not grinding poverty and certainly a cut above my father's station in life. I have found, for example, no formal photographs of my father and his family – I doubt if it was a practice they could afford – but my mother is recorded in a series of photographs from infancy to young womanhood. She is always well – indeed, smartly – dressed, whether in formal studio poses, in school class groups (one in fancy dress), or sitting by a hedge or lolling in the sun on the beach, perhaps at Porthgwarra or Lamorna. All the children had a good schooling; the boys sang in the cathedral choir. (My uncle George was an accomplished musician and in later life earned a living, or at least his whisky, playing the piano in West Coast pubs when he tried his luck on the goldfields. My brother, serving with the navy in the Pacific during the Second World War, came across him playing honky-tonk piano in a Suva bar.) My mother and her siblings all holidayed with their west country relatives, including the four unmarried cousins at Boscarne; it is likely that they and others supported the fatherless family.

The second death in my mother's family, that of her brother Will, came in 1917 on the Western Front, less than six months before she was married. The chaplain wrote to his mother: 'He was in charge of a party of seven which had been sent back from the trenches to fetch water. It was about seven in the evening. As they were going away from the lines a shell burst in the midst of them and killed your dear son.' The family has preserved a more bitter memory – that Will had protested that it was a moonlit night and the Germans would surely see them; they did. His photograph, in army uniform, on the Makino Road wall showed a soft-looking, round-faced young man, hardly more than a boy in looks if not in years, the ghostly image of an uncle who had never had the chance to become one.

My widowed grandmother, her two daughters married and her surviving son a roving bachelor, became a member of the Makino Road household in 1921 or 1922, between the births of my sister and my brother. I doubt if my mother, always an independent person, would have sent for her; it is more likely that she simply announced that she intended to come. Though she was a hard worker and undoubtedly earned her keep in and around the house, she also became a source of discontent and disruption. It is easy to see how, widowed with four children to bring up and managing to bring them up well, she would have been used to running things. After my mother's long-delayed but inevitable quarrel with her, she removed to a private hotel at Plimmerton, where I enjoyed beach holidays as a child. Late in life she returned to the family, by now in Dannevirke, and died there.

The story my mother told of her first New Zealand experience was one of shock and grief. The troopship berthed at Auckland, perhaps in darkness for she did not speak of the town itself; they boarded the overnight train south, the 'Limited', so called because it stopped at only a limited number of stations, one of which was Feilding, where they were to be set down in the early morning. At something like 2 a.m. she woke in her second class seat by the window, raised the blind and looked out on a ghostly moonlit landscape of white stumps and skeletal tree trunks. It appalled her; she lay back in her seat and wept for the neat fields and hedges of Cornwall.

I am not sure that she was ever quite at home in New Zealand. She had grown up in Truro, a compact small city dominated by its neo-Gothic cathedral, with much of its Georgian architectural heritage intact. She had holidayed out west with her cousins in their stone farm houses and walked along the cliff-top paths from one golden sanded cove to another nestling between granite headlands. She spoke often of a ring of standing stones on a cousin's field, the Merry Maidens, reputed to have been turned to stone for dancing on a Sunday. Her father and her brother were buried in Truro, close to the Kenwyn parish church; relatives and ancestors were scattered through the churchyards of the west country. While for her husband history came out of books and shaped his response to the times he lived through, for her it was the environment all about her – the cathedral spire, the observances of the church, the quiet river flowing from Truro to Falmouth, the immemorial fields, paths, cottages and great houses, the Merry Maidens forever at their dance. In New Zealand she was acutely aware of their absence; still, from her remembrance of them, this history became the inheritance of a colonial generation, her children. Not that she pined for the country she had left; she was a domestic person and made a home in a weatherboard house with a corrugated iron roof on a metalled road alongside the railway, one of a straggling line of dwellings not in the least resembling a village, surrounded not by fields and hedges but by paddocks and wire fences.

Towards the end of her long life – she lived to be ninety-three – she returned in mind to her beloved Cornwall, before she took refuge in the total silence of her final years. Sitting in her chair in the 'home', she would talk in a lively manner of the places and scenes of her youth, especially in and around Truro. It took a while to realise that this was where she believed she was – the Infirmary was just over the hill (there was no hill), the sea was a little way off (it was far distant). Pathetic? Perhaps, but a real return of the native in every way except physical presence, and that was coming to matter less and less. Earlier, she had often spoken of the pranks she and her friends had got up to during the long summer evenings – young women quite evidently having something of a high old time. I formed the notion that in her very old age she returned to the brief period of freedom she had enjoyed before her long life of family service began.

In other ways she was probably quite content with her new country – certainly she was aware that she had been brought to a place that was good for her because it was good for her family. When, after three years at Oxford and my degree close to finished, I wrote home to say that if I could get a job I would stay on in the United Kingdom, she reproached me with some sharpness for deserting the country that had given me my chances. Maybe her not-at-homeness was nostalgia, long-lasting and powerful enough but not to be confused with the real world. For her, too, the old world was where opportunities were withheld and injustices inflicted. She often spoke of the way her dead brother had been deprived of a scholarship because of a physical defect – not, however, one severe enough to keep him out of the army – and of how her own success at school and her pleasure in learning had been cut short when she had to go to work. She enjoyed at least one new opportunity; she learned to drive and took the Model T everywhere, on business as well as pleasure trips.

I think she had a wonderful skill at making do with what she had, probably learned from her mother during the difficult years before and after her father's death and from her own hard-working life as a child and a young woman. Not that she was at first skilled in the domestic arts; when she was married she did not know, as she put it, how to boil water. In her new country she had to manage in a wooden house on an acre of land reaching back to the farmlands, with well-established fruit trees – damsons and a sloe, yellow plums and cherry plums, apples and pears, gooseberries, cape gooseberries, raspberries and loganberries. They seem, if only in memory, to have been there for ever and always laden with fruit. There was also a large back area left more or less alone; this, with the farmland and the little stream behind the section and the hill pastures with a surviving stretch of bush over the railway line, was the domain of my childhood.

The house and the land were a work place as well as a place to live. A good deal of the space was taken up by a small poultry farm – ramshackle wire-netting-faced sheds for the fowls, movable enclosures for young birds, and a stoutly built and windowless shed with rows of incubators heated by kerosene lamps. This enterprise, nostalgically called Lamorna Poultry Farm, required a great amount of intensive work and much of it, maybe most, was done by the women and some by the children. My father did the heavy work around the house and land and brought home his wage packet – supposedly unopened but not invariably so. I remember him carefully turning the rows of eggs in the incubators (a drop in temperature meant a failure to hatch), working the hand-driven chaff-cutter for green food, killing (by a deft movement breaking the neck) the table birds and eviscerating them – 'inside-outing' we called it, and we would rush to watch while he was at work. But the women did the plucking and the singeing (to remove the small fluffy feathers) and the dressing for sale.

The work on the poultry farm was unremitting – feeding the birds, collecting the eggs, cleaning them and packing them for the local market and for further afield. There were seasonal tasks, too – packing the 'day-old chicks' into perforated shoe boxes and despatching them by rail to customers, preserving eggs with a mixture brewed in the washday copper (I think this was a failure), trundling the two miles to and from Feilding in the Model T with produce for sale and supplies of feed. I have one memory of especial delight. The chicks not sold off as day-old were raised in wire enclosures; the infertile eggs were hard-boiled and we loved to feed them to the gangling and ravenous young birds. Perhaps two or three times during the year selected birds – White Leghorns, Silver Wyandottes, Rhode Island Reds and other forgotten breeds – were taken to A&P shows in nearby towns, often to win prizes and ribbons and to be pictured in the paper. Once a year dressed poultry was prepared for the produce stall at the Methodist church fund-raiser in the Feilding drill hall. It was a matter of family pride that quite substantial sums were raised in this way for the church – more, I suspect, a matter of holding a place on the social scale than of helping the church in its mission.

Religious activity was a regular but uncertain matter. We children went to the Methodist Sunday school; our parents, each with a personal ambiguity, attended the Methodist church, at least from time to time. My father probably found some difficulty in reconciling his church with his deification of humanity. My mother's ambivalence, I can now see, was of a different kind. Her family had been Church of England with High Church leanings, unlike her west country relatives, firm Methodists when I encountered them; she remained of that persuasion while going to the Methodist church for the sake of family unity. Later in life, after her children had grown up (and all ceased to be in any noticeable way Methodist), she went back to the Church of England, and confided to me that she had always found the Methodists more like a club than a church.

At my baptism I was given the middle name 'Hosking', as had my brother three years earlier. That was, of course, my mother's maiden name and passing it on to children was not unusual. But I have been led to believe that something else was going on, at my grandmother's instigation. The Cornish relatives, especially the family of two brothers and two sisters who lived (bachelors and spinsters to the end) at Boscarne, were in this way being given a signal that some antipodean cousins should be remembered in their wills. My mother, too, had her own designs on the inheritance; she had let it be known that she would be glad to be left their stamp collection, reputed to contain a Penny Black and other rarities. Neither hint proved of any avail, but in fact these relations did not forget us. From time to time my mother would receive a letter with an English pound note in it; and every Christmas a large package arrived from Boscarne with something for everybody.

In the early 1950s my wife Dorothy and I stayed with my cousin John Williams and his family at Roskestal, the farm where my mother had often holidayed. He was a lovely man, devoted to his Methodist chapel and his male voice choir; it was easy to believe the story that he and my mother had been keen on each other in their early years. The second of the rich Boscarne relatives died while we were there. At the house after the funeral, one of the two who were left, Thomasine, a tiny lady, greeted my tall wife with the remark 'My, you have grown', and the other, Willie, a wispy old man, scared the daylights out of me by leading out his prize bull on the end of what seemed to me a piece of string. We had gone from Boscarne to the parish church at St Buryan on foot, in a long procession through the country lanes. The entire (Anglican) service was spoken by the parish priest with his wife making the responses; as all these people were Methodist they took no part.

Being kin I was placed close to the head of the procession, after the women in black gossiping away with their hands held over their eyes in grief. My wife, non-kin, was placed well back towards the end. My uncle Will, married to my mother's sister, Janie, later told us of his outrage at having been treated in the same way on a similar occasion. He too, a labouring man who felt that the world in general had treated him badly, had cherished hopes of finding a place in the will and was angered to find that it was not so. Wealthy, indeed, they had been; when, years later, the last of them had gone, desk drawers were found to be stuffed with cheques not only uncashed but drawn upon banks that no longer existed. Or so some of my less well-to-do Cornish cousins believed; they, too, had failed to find a place in the will. There were dark mutterings about those who had.

No manna fell from heaven, especially not in New Zealand during the depression. The poultry farm failed, leaving debt behind – the figure of £100, huge it seemed then, owed to the Farmers' Co-op for stock feed, sticks in my mind. Then there were the Angora rabbits. Something had to be done with the sheds emptied by the unprofitable fowls, many of whom had been eaten. The white fluffy rabbits grew wool which was shipped off, again in shoe boxes, to Paton and Baldwin in England – that is, until the bottom fell out of the knitting wool market. Once again there was work for the women, shearing the creatures with household scissors on the kitchen table – I recall vividly their red eyes gleaming as they were shorn. There were prizes to be won in shows – prizes also for a short-haired greyish mottled variety, Chinchillas perhaps, kept just for show purposes. Again there was a business failure; this time the rabbits were buried in mass graves, not eaten.

My father was of a sanguine disposition but prone to depression as each high hope ended in failure. Next, he was drawn to hydroponics, seduced by a plausible salesman, but was dissuaded by the example of a friend being swindled; they were Bible people, and I recall the loser lugubriously quoting 'I was a stranger and you took me in.' My father had earned a wage, of course, from regular employment in the timber yard for most of the 1920s, and then, after the depression cost him that job, from seasonal employment in the freezing works. In those days working families often looked to some domestic enterprise for a second source of income, commonly earned by the women of the household. When that collapsed about the same time as my father went on strike and lost his freezing works job, the household income dwindled to the meagre dole.

The hard times were all around us too, but thanks to my mother we ate better, were better clad, were better sheltered and kept warmer than many of our contemporaries. This, I feel sure, was one of my mother's great gifts. She was a true carer; I do not remember ever being cold or hungry even when very little money was coming in. I have only one memory of unhappiness – a frugal mid-depression birthday. I burst into tears and said that I had never had such a miserable birthday. My mother, too, began to cry and said that she and my brother had tried hard to make it happy.

There were also depression Christmases when the RSA came around with toys; I did not mind this a bit, but my mother found it an indignity.

We certainly ate well. Milk was plentiful, and every day my mother made Cornish clotted cream in a wide pan slowly heated and left to stand overnight. Butter came cheaply from the dairy factory and meat from the freezing works. Potatoes, vegetables and much fruit we grew – other fruit, like oranges and bananas, were bought at marked-down prices as 'specks' from the Chinese fruiterer in Feilding. My mother became an excellent cook in the Cornish way: thick heavy pastry made with lard, apple pies, pasties, yeast buns, heavy cake, potato cake, saffron buns and cake (tiny packets of saffron came in letters from Cornwall), seedy cake made with caraway seeds. We took good lunches to school, sandwiches and cake, no doubt – but chiefly I recall the delicious apple pasties. But vegetables were a different matter; for the whole of my childhood I fought a drawn battle over done-to-death greens.

We remained decently dressed through the depression years – two photographs from the mid 1930s show my sister in a good dress and my brother and me in dark suits (with long trousers) and ties. I recall mine with distaste; it was cut down from an adult suit and fitted almost nowhere. I was at the end of a hand-me-down chain and, to my acute embarrassment, for a while had to wear to school a pair of girl's shoes with a buttoned strap across the instep. For my mother, hard times would have reinforced her zeal for respectability. My father, whose chief response was political action, was ready to sail a little closer to the wind. Once they had a severe difference of opinion about right and wrong. Together with neighbours he proposed to remove, at night, some unused railway sleepers from beside the line. She protested that it was not honest and he that it was honest but still had to be done at night. And she: 'If it's honest why does it have to be done at night?' Did she remember, perhaps, the unsavoury reputation of her Cornish ancestors? Not wreckers, exactly, but ready to take advantage of the bounty of the sea; as late as my own time among them, there were tales of valuable items washed up in the cove and appropriated – at night, of course.

My father was nonetheless distinctly respectable. He seldom drank alcohol, smoked frugally (a two-ounce tin a week of flake pipe tobacco rolled into cigarettes, a habit I for a time imitated), brought his pay packet home and was given his 'baccy money', was wonderfully kind to his children (I remember him hitting me only once, with a thin piece of wood on the bottom, and it was a terrible experience), severely disapproved of extramarital sexual activities, and was not given to quarrelling even when he felt he was getting a raw deal. Once, when he was getting a bad time from my mother for offering a critical comment, he exclaimed 'I wish I could bite my tongue out!'

Politics took my father out of the house a good deal; he enjoyed the activity for its own sake and, as he later let it be known, as an escape from the domestic tyranny of women, the formidable mother–daughter combination he discovered that he had married. 'A stranger in my own house' was his phrase. But my mother loyally supported my father's activity in the Labour Party. When, in 1938, we left Feilding for Dannevirke, a farewell function was put on by the party in the drill hall. I do not know what was presented to my father, but I know that my mother received a pretty table lamp. 'What', I asked her, cheekily, 'have you done for the Labour Party?' She, self-deprecatory as usual, agreed that she had done nothing. But my father was emphatic: 'She kept me going!' A well-merited reproach; in fact she kept us all going.

We were a fairly healthy lot, though my brother suffered constantly from catarrh. There was a family doctor, a surly man reputed to resent having to attend 'lodge' patients for a reduced fee from the friendly society. I was born at home and delivered into the world by the midwife, as were my sister and brother. My only trip to hospital was for the then routine extraction of adenoids and tonsils – there was a 'tonsil' day in the Palmerston North public hospital, with a row of anaesthetised children and the surgeon moving swiftly down the line, snipping off and passing on. (Surely not? But it was held to be so, and perhaps it was.) Only one serious medical condition affected my early life. My father was operated on for a hernia, then commonly called a 'rupture', and almost died from his unsuspected haemophilia; he recalled, too late, having had a very bad time many years before when he had his teeth out. It was a frightening experience for all of us.

People at that time expected less of medical services, and certainly traditional remedies were still about. My mother kept a 'medicine chest' (a small cupboard on the bathroom wall): iodine and peroxide for cuts and grazes; cascara, the great specific against constipation; quinine, perhaps for feverish colds; witchhazel, I suppose for bruises and contusions; friar's balsam for inhalations. She dispensed these with a firm but compassionate hand – both needed, for iodine or peroxide on a raw cut really hurt. She was dragooned into rubbing liniment into the limbs of Mrs Kelso next door, to relieve sciatica, a complaint from which she suffered herself. A number of childhood illnesses were survived with rest and little else; maybe you just waited and hoped when you fell ill. Scarlet fever was a feared scourge but it did not come our way; mumps, measles and chicken pox did.

It was a good home and an interesting neighbourhood. On one side were Mr and Mrs Kelso, an Irish couple reputed to drink too much – it was said that when they visited a relative on the other side of the ranges, the horse brought them back along the tricky unfenced Manawatu Gorge road sound asleep in the gig. Beyond them lived a bachelor Scot of genteel pretensions (a room full of blue and white china and lampshades with glass pendants), Mr Mickie, who looked nostalgically back to better days in the old country in the service of unspecified members of the royal family. Further down the road was a Seventh Day Adventist couple who had nothing to do with anybody and could be seen at their front gate on Saturday evening watching the sun go down over the hill so that they could work furiously during the remaining daylight. Or so it was said. On the other side were the Wiltons. My father and the husband were Bill and Arch, but the two women were Mrs Oliver and Mrs Wilton to each other and as such remained close friends into old age, long after we had left the district. Our school friends lived on the other side of the dairy factory. We trailed to school with them, built Guy Fawkes bonfires with them (old tyres from the dairy factory trucks at the core), roamed the hills and the more distant patch of bush with them, fought battles with supplejack bows and toi toi arrows, dammed and diverted the creek in the paddocks behind us. With hard-working parents, we were on our own a good deal and came, as far as I can recall, to little harm – unless, indeed, a surreptitious cigarette now and then, leading to a not-quite-lifetime addiction, has to be taken into account.

None of us had any doubt about the importance of education. But our chances were not evenly distributed. I was lucky enough to turn ten as the depression drew to an end in 1935; I stayed in the education system for most of the rest of my life. My sister was more or less automatically routed into 'Commercial' at high school, and around the age of fifteen found employment as a shorthand-typist. My brother was sent off – by train fourteen miles each way – to the 'Tech' at Palmerston North to take trade courses; after a couple of years he began work as an apprentice. Each had cherished aspirations which went well beyond the ration of education they were allowed; this inclined them to think that I had all the luck and, if only for a time (I hope), to resent it.

While I enjoyed primary school, my interest in history, in a book-learning sense, did not begin in the classroom. My father had acquired a multi-volume set of the *Harmsworth History of the World* and the first volume of an illustrated history of the First World War. These, together with *Mother Goose's Fairy Tales* (luridly illustrated), were my childhood reading. Before I could read, I turned the pages of these volumes devouring the illustrations, for the most part vivid anecdotal portrayals – Hannibal crossing the Alps, Napoleon looking back to the French coast from the deck of the *Bellerophon*, German soldiers in their trenches being blown sky high by mines, Allied soldiers inquiring of French peasants 'Have you seen the Uhlans pass this way?' No social studies here, but the grandeur and the pity of human striving and suffering.

We were a reading family; here, too, the example was set by my mother who had the great skill of being able to read while knitting socks on four steel needles. I remember winter nights with all of us sitting around a good wood fire reading in silence (my father was probably out at a meeting). The books included the many prizes won at Sunday school for knowing the Bible well. They were of the English public school variety – *Blake of the Modern Fifth*, *The School Across the Road* and that moralistic Victorian classic, *Eric, or Little by Little*. There was also a wireless, built by my mother's brother, who appeared from time to time during his travels bringing gifts.

But we remained a people of the book. School did little more than build upon this foundation, especially through that useful volume with Cook on the cover, *Our Nation's Story*. In Standard 4 or 5 we were set to write an essay and I confidently began 'As a boy, Captain James Cook ...' and went on to tell of his experiences on the docks of Whitby. A teacher thought it could not have been honestly done, and I was set down to do it again under close supervision. I confidently began 'As a boy, Captain James Cook .... ' No more was heard of the episode.

All these historical influences were less important than the lessons learned out of school, lessons provided by the distant but vividly present country my parents remembered. I was constantly aware of a host of people to whom I was closely related who lived there; three of my grandparents were either living or buried there. Once I counted up: I found I had seven relations in New Zealand (there were a few more but I did not know about them). It would never have occurred to me to try to count the multitude in Cornwall. Letters flowed into the house, mostly from my mother's family but some from my father's sister Maggie in Fraddon. Regularly, too, came copies of *The West Briton and Cornwall Advertiser*, a fat newspaper pored over for local news and gossip. And for humour, too; the small ads stimulated my father's fond amusement at old-world quaintness – a 'nanny in milk' offered for sale often entertained him. But embedded deeper still in my awareness of the world were the stories of Cornish life, some harsh, some engaging, that I heard from both parents.

In this, too, my parents differed. 'Cornishness' had been deliberately put on one side by my self-colonising father. History, as it was found in books, encouraged him to generalise his local and personal experience into a broader English or even near-universal destiny. My mother, for her part, had a clear idea of the distinctiveness of her inheritance. We learned from her that Cornwall was 'near England', that the Tamar was a kind of international frontier, that Cornwall was 'the Delectable Duchy' with a life of its own and a proud history. It had once even had a language of its own and its last 'native speaker', Dolly Pentreath, had died in the eighteenth century. She honoured the county motto, 'One and all'; she would recite with pride 'And shall Trelawney die? / Twenty thousand Cornishmen will know the reason why'. At that time I did not know who Trelawney was, but that did not matter; it was heroic, it was history.

There are fewer surviving photographs of my mother as a young married woman than from her single years. The earliest, a studio portrait taken soon after the birth of my sister in 1920, with her in long white garments, was sent to Cornwall 'with love and best wishes to "granny"'. Granny, looking as formidable as I recall her, was on the spot before the next pictures, still posed but snapped outside the Makino Road house. My seated mother is surely pregnant with my brother in one, and in another he is on my grandmother's knee with my mother standing very upright behind her. My father is dressed in suit and tie, balding fast, lean and energetic, but strained – a self-respecting working man. I treasure one group photograph especially. In it my mother's abundant dark hair is falling down her back – I recall it always in a bun. She is wearing a dark suit or dress, quite long and with a bright floral collar and cuffs – as I remember her on formal occasions she was always more soberly dressed in her 'best navy'. She has here, unusually, a little more than a half-smile; she is altogether beautiful. The image of that capable woman, firm and kindly, disapproving when she thought the occasion required it and invariably a strong presence, is the one I have in my mind much of the time.

CHAPTER THREE

Making a Better World

For a decade, from the early 1930s to the early 1940s, my father determinedly strove for political office, three times offering himself for selection as a Labour candidate and twice standing for the party. However, the only official position he ever held (until becoming a JP late in life) was membership of the Feilding Unemployment Committee towards the end of 1932. These committees, under the auspices of the local mayor, administered unemployment relief. The one meeting at which his presence was recorded discussed the 'stand-down week', a device by which relief work was rationed out (and pay as well, for 'no pay without work' was the rule). The meeting was held in November; during that month the freezing works dispute was under way, and he would have been one of the unemployed whose lives were being regulated. The Labour Party was holding euchre evenings to raise funds for the out-of-work freezing workers, and he was the local secretary of their union. He was soon to suffer himself from the rationing of relief work. The quota varied – generally work was provided for three days a week for three weeks out of four.

Possibly he had been involved in Labour politics from as early as 1913, when a 'largely attended' meeting of the Feilding branch of the United Labour Party was reported. The ULP, moderate and respectable, closer to the Liberal tradition than to doctrinaire socialism, would have suited him well. He was a man of emphatic political opinions; the slogan 'Agitate, Educate, Legislate' was often on his lips, but he had little time for militant direct action. His notebooks show that he had some acquaintance with Marxism; however, he believed in the ballot box as the way to achieve power. He called himself a socialist and he took pride in being a working man, but class consciousness did not exclude other loyalties; he was also a firm patriot, of both the British and the New Zealand kind (a difference not significant to him). This outlook, a body of values and beliefs rather than an ideology, took shape in his mind as he matured through the experiences of emigration, employment, education and war.

In 1917, when he was twenty-seven, he began to paste news clippings into a blue-covered 'Albion Exercise Book' – it gives on its back cover such arcane information as 'Hay and Straw Weight' and 'Cloth Measure'. The clippings include his own four letters to the editor of an unnamed Cornish newspaper, perhaps the *West Briton*. Other clippings also have a radical ring – 'Labour in Revolt', for example. While his letters proudly proclaim his sense of identity with his adopted country, he emphasises his Cornish birth and upbringing in order to establish his right to be heard in his home county. Here are the first signs of political activity, but there must have been many earlier discussions on the job and in camp.

The first letter, of 30 March 1917, is headed 'A Reply to the Conscientious Objector. What a New Zealander thinks.' The 'C.O.' is dealt with severely, especially for saying that most soldiers did not know what they were fighting for. This prompts a proud assertion of the common man's, especially the colonial common man's, sense of historical purpose: 'We do know what we are fighting for, or we should not have left our new-made homes in that sunny clime under the southern cross, and spilt blood like water on the bleak shores of Anzac or the Somme.' The pride of the colonial is still a pride in being British: 'The citizen army has come into being because Briton's [sic] honour was at stake, because in the very bone of the Anglo-Saxon race there is embedded the very spirit of freedom and right.'

His religious position had already become ambiguous: his humanistic radicalism had not quite displaced traditional beliefs; perhaps it never fully did. There is a cryptic but revealing passage prompted by a comment on whether ministers should or should not smoke. Such matters were still a moral (rather than a health) issue among Methodists as late as the 1940s: when some of us in the Bible class caught our minister smoking a pipe in his study, he guiltily put it away. In 1917 my father dismissed such matters as 'petty differences'. 'To me the teaching of the Peasant of Galilee has been garbled and distorted until we have a net work of creeds and religious dogmas from which some men peep and cover themselves with the mantle of a crucified Christ.' The 'net work', perhaps, is a trap from which people need to be liberated, and the 'mantle' the misuse of the gospel for self-regarding ends. He is, I think, shifting towards the view that creeds and dogmas obscure the essential social core of the gospel.

He was a Methodist local preacher after the war – I grew up believing that he came from a long line of local preachers but I have no evidence of this – taking services in small country centres around Feilding. That lasted for only a few years; he had a sharp difference of opinion with a conservative lawyer who was influential in the church, no doubt over political matters. He ceased to serve what he had come to regard as a hypocritical institution which betrayed its founder by not recognising the socialism of the Sermon on the Mount. In his old age he took up the office again in Dannevirke and proved to be a popular preacher. In country districts people would show up in some numbers to his services. I suspect that he talked rather more than he preached, reflecting on stories from his life's experiences. I doubt if there was much theology in his sermons.

While the radicalism of these early letters was real, their patriotic fervour was just as strong: it is in Britain that the surge of democracy and the rise of labour will take place. There is also an echo of Woodrow Wilson and the Versailles reconstruction of Europe into national entities: 'The world will be reconstructed not by drawing straight lines across the map, but by racial ties, the ties that bind and hold above all others.' But class, rather than nationality, mattered most when he looked to the condition of his country of origin. He called himself 'an uneducated farm labourer' whose 'father was one before me'. At the heart of his attack upon the condition he aptly described as 'advanced serfdom' lies the issue of property in land. 'We, as a class, have lost the control over the first essential of our existence. Why has the land been converted into private property? Our forefathers driven from the soil to give solitude to the landlord's pheasants?' Another passage, from a letter replying to 'Fair Play', exemplifies his patriotic radicalism on the eve of his return to New Zealand: 'We have listened for years to the advice of those who have never soiled their hands with manual toil. Some of us have been farm labourers in Cornwall, and as boys worked for 8*d.* a day. And the men who count in the ranks of labour are not those who ... never did an honest day's toil in their lives. The men who represent true, solid labour are from our ranks – men who have toiled and studied the conditions under which they live.' He makes his claim, on grounds of experience and understanding, to be an enlightened working man.

Upon his return to New Zealand in 1919 he found a unified Labour Party with a small but vigorous body of MPs and the firm intention of achieving social justice by democratic process; industrial action had been tried in the strikes of 1912 and 1913 and had failed. Hopes ran high but their fulfilment was long deferred. In successive elections Labour's fortunes ebbed and flowed, but came nowhere near success. Its leader, Harry Holland, despaired of ever getting into power – and, indeed, he never managed to, dying two years before the long-postponed triumph of 1935. I feel sure that my father anticipated each election with high hopes and contemplated the results with deep gloom.

Early twentieth century Feilding, a small town in the heart of a rich farming district, was not a likely springboard for an aspiring Labour politician. And yet it was not unrewarding; he achieved an eminence in the local Labour movement that might have eluded him in a larger place. Though he failed in his great ambition to become a Member of Parliament, once his disappointment was over he took comfort from his part in the victory of 1935. He believed that the peaceable revolution had happened and had remade the country. When Labour eventually lost power in 1949, he consoled himself with the belief that the enemy had been converted to the Labour programme, especially social security, and that there would be no reversal of direction. Little happened, before his death in 1967, to undermine that conclusion.

By the time I remember my father clearly, his political career was well-established. He was chairman of the Oroua electorate Labour Representation Committee, a regular delegate to the party's annual conferences, a regional representative on the party's Dominion Council (a largely honorific position but one of some standing) and, in 1935, the party's parliamentary candidate for Oroua. He was known to the party's leaders; when, in the early 1960s, I talked to Walter Nash while Eve Page was painting his portrait (this was because he would not stop talking and Eve needed a break to get on with the painting), I found that he remembered the older Bill Oliver, if a little uncertainly.

He became locally notorious as well as prominent during the freezing works dispute of 1932. This was not strictly a strike, for the dispute surfaced in the off-season. The workers who rejected the proposed introduction of the new chain slaughtering system were determined not to accept employment for the killing season which was to open towards the end of the year. My father knew very well that this was futile, with thousands already unemployed, but after strenuously arguing against the action he stood with his fellows in the name of solidarity. The employers hired new men – I learned to know such strike-breakers as 'scabs' – and there was a little violence in the streets of Feilding between them and the strikers. Years later, after we had moved to Dannevirke, he and other strikers met with the 'new' workers for a ceremonial 'burying of the hatchet' – so he described it, and I had the impression that a real hatchet had been buried.

I have one vivid memory of the dispute, perhaps the only episode which involved the whole family – the visit of a policeman to serve a notice instructing my father to desist from speaking in the streets. The policeman was a good friend of his; later I came to realise that he was Louis Johnson's father. I can still recall his navy-blue legs striding down the path, my mother's anxiety and the obscure fright we felt at this sudden manifestation of the law. In those days a police summons was known as a 'bluey', from the colour of the paper on which the legal form was then printed; as boys we had a healthy fear of being summonsed, maybe for buying cigarettes and smoking them in the park. That day we believed, incorrectly, that a 'bluey' had been served on my father for his part in the strike.

He was a powerful speaker – too powerful for some occasions; he treated a small handful of people in a country hall as if they were the Friday night crowds in Feilding he used to address from a soapbox (probably a butter or a kerosene box). His eloquence was not restricted to political meetings. He was also in some demand for his recitations: Kipling's 'If' was a favourite and Browning's 'Incident of the French Camp', with its ringing first line 'You know, we French stormed Ratisbon'. There was a small corrugated iron community hall at Makino Road. I remember one occasion when the announcement was made that 'Mr Oliver will oblige' and he did, with an impassioned recitation. I recall, too, a debate on a forgotten topic, possibly at a meeting of the Feilding WEA, at which my father's opponent, an enormously large service-station operator known to everyone, especially irreverent kids, as 'Fatty Guy', was demolished by my father shouting repeatedly 'Heil Hitler' when the speaker asserted that anyone who believed in – what? – 'should be put up against a wall and shot', until the speaker was overcome with helpless laughter.

I went with my father in the Model T on Sunday afternoons to meetings of the Oroua Labour Representation Committee. I usually wandered around the small centres, Halcombe, Hunterville, Sanson, Kimbolton, Rongotea, while the meeting was going on – perhaps this was his share of child minding? It was driving in the Model T that I heard the secretary of the LRC say in all seriousness: 'You know, Bill, I've thought about it and come to the conclusion that anyone who does not agree with us is either a bigot or a fool.' As solemnly, my father agreed. Labour MPs stayed in the house from time to time on speaking engagements. And, because it was a quarrel of sorts and that was pretty rare, I clearly recall my mother protesting when my father called J. G. Cobbe, the local MP and a Cabinet minister, also pillar of the Methodist church, 'a dirty' – or was it a 'wicked'? – 'old man', and my father insisting that that was what he was 'politically'.

In 1935 my father stood for the Labour Party in a rural electorate with only one town of any size, Feilding. The studio portrait taken for publicity purposes shows a handsome middle-aged man – he was forty-five – with a high-domed forehead, deep sunken eyes and a markedly sober expression. The Coalition candidate was the sitting member, Cobbe, and there was also a Democrat, Ernest Fair, a draper and former mayor. This was a small town and there were some social difficulties. The Cobbe children, grandsons of the sitting member, were quite close contemporaries at school and Sunday school. More difficult for me, however, was the 'civics' lesson conducted by my teacher, no doubt well-intentioned but acutely disconcerting to the ten-year-old identified as the son of one of the candidates. I suppose it was meant to make the election real for the class; it was made altogether too real for my comfort. My sister, at high school, had more to put up with, so my father told me years later.

A big meeting I attended was not at all embarrassing, for I sat at the back of the dress circle in one of the two local cinemas. It was addressed by three Labour candidates, my father, C. L. Hunter for Manawatu and the improbable Labour candidate for Rangitikei, Ormond Wilson. He was a scion of the pastoral elite, not long returned from Oxford; I was to know him slightly and rather uneasily in later life as an historian. I remember the young Wilson's dangling forelock and his well-rounded patrician syllables – 'a voice like a rolling river', as Hubert Witheford was later to say. But chiefly I remember my father's resonant trumpet notes bouncing off the vaulted ceiling of the theatre. In the same theatre, I enjoyed hearing John A. Lee, whose voice could also easily fill a large space.

Less appropriately, my father's powerful voice sounded forth at a meeting in Utiku held in one of those tiny halls set down in the middle of nowhere. The small room was occupied by only a dozen or so dour-looking country men. At question time one man began 'If a Labour government is elected . . . .' My father, with perhaps unconscious theatricality, leapt to his feet and corrected him: 'Not "if", my friend, "when".' The questioner looked anything but convinced and in fact quite irritated, but went on with his question. So sanguine was my father's temperament in that heady time that he reckoned he had secured around twenty-five votes that night, from all those present and, of course, from their wives.

The 1935 election was a complex affair. The Coalition, formed earlier by the merging of the Reform and United parties, campaigned as a single party; it was to become the National Party after its defeat. A right-wing revolt against what were taken to be the socialistic policies of the Coalition brought Democratic Party candidates into the running; in Oroua as elsewhere there was a three-way contest. My father had high hopes, both for the success of Labour as a whole and for his own prospects. Labour won handsomely, but his expectation of a personal victory was dashed. He came a rather distant second in spite of polling well (but still not first) in Feilding, which afforded him some consolation. For reasons that remain obscure, the one booth in the entire electorate that placed him first was Ohingaiti. It must have irked him that Wilson and Hunter were returned for Labour (by a whisker in Hunter's case) in the neighbouring rural electorates, thanks to the Democrat candidates splitting the opposition vote. But in Oroua, an overwhelmingly rural electorate, Cobbe was returned with a comfortable majority.

Oroua vanished with the redrawing of electoral boundaries in 1937; Manawatu and Rangitikei had sitting Labour members, a rare condition that did not survive the 1938 election. So, for that election, my father threw his hat into the ring in Pahiatua, on the other side of the Tararua range. The party selected a Wairarapa farmer, George Hansen, but my father was appointed paid organiser for the election, in an effort to topple the sitting member, E. A. Ransom, another who had been a minister in the Coalition. My father opened an office in Dannevirke's High Street and slept in the back room.

He was once again away from home but that was no novelty. After 1935 he had worked on farms, eradicating thistles and harvesting, been a census sub-enumerator riding around the district on a small motorcycle, and dug ditches on the little airfield close to Feilding. Then, with the expansion of public works initiated by the new government after 1935, he found work on the Saddle Road at Wharite, an alternative to the frequently blocked Manawatu Gorge route. Here he lived for the week in a Public Works tent camp, coming home for weekends. The tents, half-timbered with corrugated iron chimneys, were (he insisted) a cut above those of the depression camps, thanks to Bob Semple. He talked a great deal of politics while he was there. He liked the companionship of men; he was not really a domestic person.

To his organiser's despair, Hansen was a stodgy candidate. My father, with his lively sense of history, tried to get his candidate to exploit the romance of his Scandinavian ancestors, the people who had within living memory tamed the Seventy Mile Bush and turned the wilderness into smiling farm land. All in vain; in vain, too, the party's calculation that it could win a rural seat with a farmer candidate, for the countryside stayed loyal to the sitting member. Too many town voters had been put off by the worthy but phlegmatic farmer – or so my father reckoned. He held that if he had been the candidate he would have swept the three towns, Dannevirke, Pahiatua and Woodville, and won. Maybe not; this electorate was soon to become Keith Holyoake's stronghold.

The 1938 election was Labour's greatest success, though not in Pahiatua. It was a high point from which the future held only the prospect of decline (but one postponed by the outbreak of war in 1939). At the same time the family's fortunes looked up; my father found work in Dannevirke as timekeeper in the local Public Works Department depot, the first 'collar and tie' job he had ever had. Public Works schemes, under the direction of the energetic Semple, were transforming the roading of the country, partly through the construction of ramps over railway lines to replace level crossings. There was, probably, a good deal of 'make-work' about the programme but it caught the public imagination – the ramps were sometimes referred to as 'Bob Semple's monuments'. For my father, there was a bit of politics here too, of an unpleasant kind: he later learned to his distress that another man had lost his job to make room for the faithful party servant.

The family moved to Dannevirke, the only shift it ever made. In the new town my mother missed her friend and neighbour, Mrs Wilton, but liked the tidy house only a mile from the town centre with a frequent bus service – a small verandahed villa with a well-established garden and many fruit trees and berries. For me it was conveniently close to Dannevirke High School, which I joined in the fourth form. There I quickly found friends, more than I had had in Feilding. I also found Saturday morning work with the town's largest butcher, covering the town and country in the delivery van and, from time to time, work in a grocery. Here I gained a useful skill, which still serves me at Christmas time, that of making neat parcels with brown paper and string.

Going to Dannevirke High School, then under the genial headmastership of E. N. Hogben, was an especially good turn of fortune. For a year at Feilding Agricultural High School I had endured the vagaries of an unreliable (and unduly celebrated) system of 'self-government', introduced by its eccentric head, L. J. Wild, who sometimes carried on so long at morning assembly that he had to end with the instruction 'first period is cancelled'. He sometimes read New Zealand poems during these discourses, and I realised for the first time that poetry was written in this country. 'Self-government', as I experienced it, was little more than a punitive system in which you were given bad marks and fatigues by your peers (duly elected as form leaders and not slow to exploit their authority) and caned by the senior boys when you had accumulated enough of them. My chief tormenter was the sixth form son of the Democrat candidate of 1935. It was, indeed, a situation of double jeopardy; teachers also used the cane and it seemed to me that they separately punished the same offences. I fell into a downward spiral of crime and punishment and began to wonder where, if ever, it would all end. Luckily it ended with my going to a school where I managed to get on to the right side of the justice system and experienced no caning and little other punishment for four enjoyable years.

From the start my father was busy in the Dannevirke branch of the Labour Party and in the electorate LRC. He was resented by some as a newcomer; certainly there were bitter struggles with a formidable lady office-holder, in which I think he did not entirely succeed. There was also a returned soldier with oratorical pretensions not unlike his own but, or so it seemed to me, of a coarser kind. I remember this man carrying on at some length about that great educational experience he and his fellows had had in going overseas in the first war, only to provoke from the back of the hall the interjection 'It was free, too, Charlie.' His son, also Charlie, became a friend of mine at school. We and a few others set up a junior Labour Party branch and ran weekly euchre nights in the newly acquired Labour Hall – an ambitious venture that never paid its way. At these euchre tourneys, local semi-professionals paid a small entry fee and competed for a cash prize. The organisers had to get enough in admission charges to make a profit after the prize of £5 and the cost of the supper had been covered. Our profits were short-lived; this was, I think, the only entrepreneurial activity I have ever undertaken.

Within a year of the family's shift to Dannevirke, the Second World War had broken out. With the non-communist left in general, my father saw in National Socialism the final capitalist effort to turn back the tide of social justice; Munich and appeasement, for him, became the crowning betrayal of the corrupt British ruling class. When, in the local cinema, a newsreel showed Neville Chamberlain making his 'peace with honour' speech on his return from Germany, my father loudly expressed the view that he should be shot. Soon after the outbreak of war he spoke at the local meeting of a nationwide campaign to persuade the Labour government, still under suspicion for its anti-war past, to bring in conscription for military service. He avoided taking an explicitly anti-party view and insisted that in supporting the change he did not speak for the party but as 'plain Bill Oliver, an ordinary working man'. He invoked a venerable Labour position by insisting that the conscription of wealth should accompany the conscription of men.

My father was a delegate to the Labour conference in 1940 and voted with the majority which expelled John A. Lee for his attacks upon the ailing Prime Minister. He venerated Savage, whose benign image beamed down from our kitchen wall, as it did in so many New Zealand homes, a photographic icon of a secular saint. He had often been a delegate before; I went with him to one conference in the later 1930s, staying in the Salvation Army People's Palace, not far from the Trades' Hall where the conference met. I sat in the gallery and saw him vainly trying to catch the chairman's eye; in this milieu public speaking was a basic skill and those who had it liked to exercise it at every opportunity. ('He's no good on his feet' was, for my father, a devastating criticism of an aspiring politician.) I remember the imposing figure of the chairman, James ('Big Jim') Roberts, farewelling a deputation from the Methodist church with the assurance that, after all, the Labour Party was doing the same work as the church in applying 'practical Christianity'. I forget what specific point the deputation had sought to make; I could see, however, that it had been smothered in rhetoric.

Of course, my father deplored the attacks on Savage, the Moses who had led the party out of the wilderness; he would have believed, too, that the stability of a troubled wartime government was at stake and that it was the duty of all good men to come to the aid of the party. (Did he use these words? Somehow they echo in the memory.) He was, for personal as well as political reasons, an out-and-out party loyalist. He deplored Lee's 'shamelessness' in writing *Children of the Poor*, which he took to be a straightforward autobiographical account. How could a decent man write that his sister had been a prostitute and, further, one who went with Chinese? (Probably the term he used was 'Chinamen', or possibly one of the yet more pejorative synonyms.) As a party organiser, he had conducted Lee around the Pahiatua electorate in 1938 – Lee was later to claim that these speaking tours had brought about the government's victory and gave him a claim upon the Cabinet position he was denied. My father was not impressed with Lee's stock opening to his speech – 'The last time I came to this town I was not welcomed by the Mayor, I was carrying my swag and sleeping rough.' He thought that it was fine on a first hearing, but palled with repetition – not that he could have heard it all that often, for there were only three towns with mayors in the electorate. Lee, in his opinion, was a 'ratbag'.

His loyalty to the men who led the Labour movement was, I came to think, altogether too uncritical. More than ten years later, during the 1951 waterfront dispute, when I ventured some criticisms of F. P. Walsh, the dominant figure in the Federation of Labour and the great foe of the watersiders, he replied that in his experience Walsh was 'a good friend of the working man'. A couple of years earlier, at the time of the 1949 referendum on peacetime conscription, I had offended him by writing an anti-conscription and anti-Fraser essay for a publication that a handful of us produced in Wellington. It was a humble cyclostyled pamphlet with a minute circulation. Someone showed it to him and gave him a hard time, for there was an essay signed 'W. H. Oliver' which attacked the Labour government. In return he gave me a hard time for not realising that this use of the name we shared could discredit him; the acquaintance who showed him the pamphlet assumed (or, more likely, pretended to assume) that my father was the author of the article. So full of my own importance had I been that it had not occurred to me that anyone might confuse the young university lecturer with the old Labour stalwart.

His view of the world was millennialist, but of a sober secular kind. A favourite among the pieces he recited (and used in election speeches as a peroration) was a passage from Tennyson's 'Locksley Hall', with its apocalyptic vision of an Armageddon fought in the skies, and its utopian vision of universal democracy thereafter:

> For I dipt into the future, far as human eye could see,
> Saw the Vision of the world, and all the wonder that would be;
>
> Saw the heavens fill with commerce, argosies of magic sails,
> Pilots of the purple twilight, dropping down with costly bales;
>
> Heard the heavens fill with shouting, and there rain'd a ghastly dew
> From the nations' airy navies grappling in the central blue;
>
> Far along the world-wide whisper of the south-wind rushing warm,
> With the standards of the peoples plunging thro' the thunder-storm;
>
> Till the war-drum throbb'd no longer, and the battle-flags were furl'd
> In the Parliament of man, the Federation of the world.

The immediate reality he believed in was the workers' New Zealand; at another remove it was Great Britain which, as the breeding ground of the race he was proud to belong to, remained central to human progress; in the future, it was a world remade in accordance with his ideals of social justice. This is a speculative reconstruction; such notions as the redemptive mission of the British race and the predictive character of the New Zealand experience were not uncommon or absurd at the time.

The Second World War, he believed, was being fought to defend this ideal; in addition it gave him an opportunity to get back into uniform. In September 1940 he enlisted with the RNZAF as a patrolman and served for the best part of the next four years – over eight years of his life as a New Zealander were spent in uniform. He was away from home again, but for most of the time quite close at Ohakea near Bulls and at Milson near

Palmerston North. My brother, who had already gone to work in the railways workshops at Lower Hutt and had there joined the Naval Volunteer Reserve, was before long serving with the RNZN; my sister, after a short time in Dannevirke, went to work in a Wellington office. For a few years only the two of us, my mother and I, were left in the Dannevirke house. This is the time when we became especially close; I recall with a lasting warmth the winter nights we spent together in front of the fire reading and talking, very affectionately.

My father feared, with many others, that darkness would fall on the world if Hitler triumphed. One morning early in the war I woke to the sound of groaning and looked out of my bedroom window to see the doubled-up figure of my father coming back from the front gate. He had collected the morning paper and learned that France had fallen. Not long after that I came back from town and said that I had seen a newspaper billboard reading 'Germany and Russia at War'. He was excited at the prospect and despatched me on my bicycle to check. Alas: it was a *Truth* billboard and the small print went on 'for oil supplies'. How little, this suggests, we depended upon radio for news at that time.

He undoubtedly enjoyed his return to life in uniform and to the company of men, and he was doing his bit in defence of the utopia already achieved in New Zealand. It was, for him, a just war and a war for justice. He took his role as a patrolman seriously, especially when he was sent on a month's training course to Harewood in the South Island. There I visited him and wondered if he would be able to manage the pressure. He did, and qualified in 'Aerodrome defence'. Many pages of a large exercise book are taken up with such topics as 'Principles of small arms defence' (against aircraft), 'Fire control' (machine guns) and 'H.E. grenade'. Others are taken up with 'Arrest and custody' and 'Airforce law'. The aspect of the patrolman's job he talked about most was dealing with young drunks returning overdue from leave and put behind bars to sober up. He was a humane gaoler, made tea for them and talked to them while they were there; he had a keen feeling for the young men on their way to combat and to danger.

Towards the end of the war, his time at Milson provided him with one great and unexpected pleasure. The corporal in charge of the guard, another of the many old soldiers recruited for this work, was found to be incapable of organising the duty roster; my father was added to the strength as acting corporal specifically for this task, and the rest of the time he spent gardening. The entrance to the aerodrome was a glory of bright flowers – dahlias especially. Here (and earlier at Ohakea) he wrote an immense number of verses in a rough kind of ballad metre, reflecting on life in general and the people about him in particular; many are preserved in the large exercise book which also contains his Harewood course notes.

The same book includes what appear to be his speech notes as the Labour candidate for Manawatu in the 1943 election. He stood as 'Cpl. W. H. Oliver, (R.N.Z.A.F.)' and was photographed in uniform for his campaign pamphlet. I was with him (it must have been a university vacation) when he was preparing the pamphlet and suggested that the fine 1935 photograph be used again. The idea (a bad one in any case) was rejected on the grounds that the photograph showed the sombre 'Bill Oliver' of the depression years. Something more reassuring was needed after eight years of Labour government. The 1943 pamphlet shows a sturdy figure in Air Force uniform, medal ribbons prominent on his chest and forage cap disguising his baldness, gazing confidently into the future.

This election was his last political fling. His main opponent was the Palmerston North lawyer (and later Speaker of the House), Matthew Oram, a formidable National Party candidate. And, as we know now and could have guessed then, it was the election in which Labour began its slide down from the 1938 peak. Nevertheless, my father was as confident of victory as ever. I was in Feilding on election night; while results were awaited I wandered around the town and heard from a shop doorway a progress report on the local radio. Oram was safely ahead. I returned to the Labour office to find that they had not heard the report. Hesitantly, I recited the numbers. 'He's beaten us then' was all my father said; I can still feel the awfulness of bringing the news, and hear the despair in his voice. It was the end of his dream of being a Member of Parliament; he had told me, I think during this campaign, that he looked forward to telling his family back in Cornwall that he was an MP – that he had reached the pinnacle of his emigrant achievement.

He still had the best part of a quarter-century ahead of him and he lived it happily, quite probably more happily than he would have had he achieved his political goal. In 1944, after two years at university, I was manpowered, ostensibly into 'essential industry' but in fact (after some manoeuvring to avoid factory work) into the public service on the staff of a parliamentary committee of inquiry into local government. For the first time in a life already much taken up with politics I was in the company of 'real' politicians, not (with exceptions) unpleasant men but people who seemed to have been transformed by some process of inner atrophy into merely public figures. This, perhaps, was the brash judgement of youth; but it did not seem to me that my father would have fitted in with them – or that, if he had, he would have remained the persistently optimistic and hopeful man I knew.

When he was discharged from the Air Force, in May 1944, he went back to the kind of work he had done in the 1920s, in a small timber mill, a survivor of the great mills which turned the southern Hawke's Bay into pasture land. Of course, he stayed in the Labour Party, but the Rotary Club and the company of its professional and business members came to mean more to him. He particularly enjoyed his role as the club's international correspondent. He sat, between spells of gardening, at his table in the sunny back porch, writing letters to fellow Rotarians the world over.

His children married and he was loved by his grandchildren. He became a JP and was appointed to the Dannevirke High School board of governors and paid especial attention to the school's grounds and gardens. He became friendly with the local MP and future National Prime Minister, Keith Holyoake. Well, why not – if the good society had been achieved and its enemies converted to the true faith? He liked to tell the story of election night in 1957, when Holyoake arrived at the Labour headquarters in Dannevirke after the defeat of the government he had led for a few weeks and went around the hall full of rejoicing Labour supporters, shaking every hand. That was the kind of gesture my father appreciated.

Years later, living in Oxford, and after walking around the places of his childhood and youth, I wrote a poem beginning 'In the Fields of My Father's Youth', an attempt to tie the two ends of my life together – the peasant Cornwall I had, through him, emerged from and the patrician Oxford I had, again through him, travelled to. I tried to express something of the mix of strangeness and familiarity I found in both. My mother fondly referred to it as 'Dad's poem' but I did not hear him express an opinion. That might have been because it contained some jaundiced and over-rhetorical reflections upon the fate of the political movement to which he had given so much of his life:

> the song of equality became a bribe
> offered abroad by immoral political apes,
> while good men reeled in the wake of procureurs.

Certainly I saw him as one of the 'good men' whose idealism had been misused by others. He may have realised that, and not liked it.

My father, in his own way, expressed something of the mood I had found in my study of the early socialist movements – a refusal to accept that the world need be as bad as it evidently was, a resolve to achieve a better world and a belief in its inevitability. He believed, I hope to the very end, that an instalment of that future had been realised and that he had had a hand in bringing it about.

CHAPTER FOUR

People of the Word

Feilding and Dannevirke were, and very likely still are, small towns of the kind that children regularly leave, looking for more variety, complexity and opportunity. While it could be thought of as an escape from their narrow confines, at the end of secondary school I would have found it harder to stay than to go. This was the traditional and accepted way of growing up. Even so, it was a turning point, a decisive movement away not just from a locality but also from a home which, however intact the affections remained, had become constricting. Going away preserved affection and relationship; there was no sense of alienation, and for many years I went home regularly in vacations and at weekends. Perhaps the existence of such an effortless rite of passage was an advantage country children enjoyed over their city fellows.

I can now see this short journey to Wellington in 1943 as the first step in a longer expedition retracing my father's emigrant path, the beginning of a movement back from the periphery to the centre – Cornwall, England and (more dimly) Europe. All through my childhood and youth the evidences of this other world lay around us in abundance. Then that world was a simple fact of life; later it developed into a sharper recognition of the network of affinities within which we lived. This reconstruction arises from a kind of double vision, one which enhances and does not obscure the thing seen; recollections of an earlier life and later perceptions of their significance interact like a pair of overlapping lenses. Memories are shaped and made intelligible only within the perspective of a present need to understand them. The past we recover is the past the present tells us to take an interest in.

All through my childhood at Makino Road, the main trunk line was just across the road from the front gate. Passenger trains thundered past every night, from Wellington to Auckland and back again; goods trains crept by throughout the day, some with a carriage or two at the end for people travelling to nearby towns, each with a long line of laden trucks, many refrigerated and carrying exports on the first stage of a long journey. In the dairy factory we saw great 56 lb blocks of butter packed into white pine boxes with the fernleaf trademark and the brand name 'Pakeha' impressed with a roller on the butter before sealing and nailing. It was going elsewhere – by rail to Wellington and by ship to Great Britain, a distant place but not a strange one, for week by week letters, newspapers and parcels arrived from aunts and cousins who lived there. In our own tiny domestic economy, the cardboard boxes of Angora wool went to England; the wages my father earned (for a time) at the freezing works were for processing animal products for export; and the mysterious 'slump' that made him unemployed came from overseas, from the machinations of men in New York and London whom we knew to be malign and to reach far in their malignity.

The little scatter of houses along Makino Road, the dairy factory and the railway siding were a focal point in a world of linkages and flows. Schooling reinforced this awareness of integration: history began with 'discovery', as Captain Cook and the *Endeavour* opened New Zealand's account by attaching it to a place half the world away. At Sunday school we sang hymns by Charles Wesley and Isaac Watt and received as prizes books set in English public schools. The origins of our neighbours were evident in their speech – England, Scotland and Ireland were next door and just down the road. The names of local settlements invoked a history of transplantation – Kimbolton, Bainesse, Peep-o-Day, Halcombe, Sanson,

Bunnythorpe, Ashhurst – as well as an earlier history we did not know – Rongotea, Taonui, Kopane, Awahuri, Kiwitea, Apiti and, of course, Makino itself.

Perhaps our lives would have been richer if we had sensed the history we did not know as well as the familiar history evident in our daily lives. We might have learned more, and taken less comfort from what we learned, if that had been so – if the conflict and interaction between the first possessors and the later dispossessors had been as present to us as our own occupation. That was not the case; all I knew of that earlier history was a story heard, probably at school, of the first inhabitants leaving the land sadly singing a song of farewell. I envisaged them walking away over the grassy hills just across the railway line.

The two worlds we inhabited were, however, rich enough. We were untroubled, too, by any thought of disjunction between the inherited world across the seas and the acquired world near at hand. It was simply a matter of looking at the immediate world through the eyes of the encompassing world and at that world through the eyes of the one close to hand. I still cannot believe that absorbing something of the great inheritance our origins offered us was in any way servile, colonialist or a distraction from the local 'reality'. Nor can I avoid the conclusion that it is better not to feel too wholeheartedly at home wherever you might be.

This dual perspective, far from making me and my kind (a dwindling group, for I am an offspring of the closing phase of the great emigrant outflow from Europe) in some way not fully New Zealanders, brings with it one of the formative New Zealand experiences, that of arrival and adaptation. I did not feel any strangeness in the presence of hillsides littered with stumps and fallen trunks, but I knew that my mother had been distressed by her first sight of that desolate countryside. Surely people from the warmer and more abundant islands of the Pacific felt the shock of an alien land as keenly as other immigrants? I have come to think of that trauma as an integral element in the ancestral heritage of all the peoples who live in this country, and one which we forget or ignore to our loss and at our peril. For to eliminate the experience of being a stranger is also to preclude a sense of belonging that stretches across oceans to places both as distant as the other hemisphere and as close as breathing. That sense is, for me, the source of the looking about and setting down which ends as history in the many forms of the written word. It is the force that, together with curiosity, adventure, boredom and restlessness, takes us back along the route of the original migrations, in a reverse diaspora. Perhaps this is an over-elaborate way of putting a simple proposition – that, whatever your life here, if you follow the traces that lie on or just under the ground, you will find yourself in other places and other times and, more, that this is a path you will be the poorer for not taking.

Quite literally, as a child I looked at the world map on the classroom wall and felt glad to be a New Zealander, and especially glad that being a New Zealander was more than belonging to the small country in the bottom right-hand corner. It was also a matter of belonging, even if in a less intimate way, to all the other places on the map coloured pink and especially to another small pink bit strategically placed at the upper centre. I knew, of course, that the little country was called Great Britain and that the rest of the pink places made up the British Empire. I did not consider that empire in terms of a civilising mission or of world dominance – although, in the dangerous 1930s, there was some comfort in what we were still able to believe was the power of Britain. It was rather a matter of being more at ease in a roomy place than in a narrow one, of not being lonely in the great world, with little more than a quantity of ocean nearby.

We all imbibed the lesson that it was our purpose to achieve a situation better than the one we were in; always, with my father around, that improvement would be political and social, but it would also be personal and individual. Whatever we did, it was not to be unskilled manual labour. My first two career ambitions were of the 'collar and tie' kind, to be a stationmaster and to be a lawyer; the former, no doubt, was prompted by the pervasive presence of the railway. I did not then know that I was following a venerable nineteenth century working-class tradition: a job with the railways was a well-trodden path to responsibility and respectability, and there was a uniform to prove it. Perhaps I sensed (subliminally) that in colonial New Zealand the railways, their stations and stationmasters were vital symbols of progress and of the presence and power of the state. I cannot attach any such historiographical speculation to the idea of becoming a lawyer, though many had followed that calling to enhance their standing and their fortunes in colonial New Zealand. I suspect that I was prompted by my father's emphatic statement that he had never known a poor lawyer – and that, too, is a statement about colonial ambition and mobility.

By the time I reached university in 1943 – the first, I think, of either ancestral line to do so – neither of these ambitions had survived. I had no particular goal, least of all of a vocational sort. Apart from a friend who intended to become a dentist, for reasons which were never clear, and another who proposed to be a farmer and would surely do so because he was a farmer's son, few of those I knew had highly specific career goals in the early 1940s. Perhaps the war was a disincentive to planning: any future was likely to be in a uniform, a destiny to be accepted if it could not be avoided. Many of us thought of going on to further education at the end of high school but that was not to be counted on. Maybe it was a not wholly unblessed time of comfortable indecision?

I was good at history but I did not, at that time, form any wish to be an historian; I doubt if I knew there was such a profession. Someone, of course, must have written the books I read, but I took their existence as simply part of the givenness of things; I cannot remember realising that there were such people as authors. I was also good at English and, if my activities suggested that I wanted to be anything in particular, it was to be a poet. Certainly I wrote a few poems in my youth; from many sources, including my father's recitations, I seem to have realised that poetry was one of the ways in which words were to be put to use. I studied the hymns sung on Sunday mornings, more for their form than their message, noting the rhyme schemes, the stanza forms, the number of syllables and stresses, the inversions resorted to for the sake of the rhymes, and puzzling over the *f*s and *p*s in the margin. These childhood habits lasted into adult church-going – I have always suffered the loneliness of the non-singing Methodist. At Sunday school it was a matter of reading the Bible and getting passages by heart to score marks and win prizes. I acquired a feeling for the rhythmical character of the Psalms and of strongly accented prose, and gained an early entry into the glories of the Authorised Version.

But it was not all as solemn as that. One small boy in the gaggle of kids who dawdled each day along the two miles from home in Makino to school in Feilding was respected for his skill in turning a rhyme on any occasion. I earned one through my inevitable nickname: 'Twist', he intoned, 'pissed on the spelling list.' There were, too, songs sung at primary school, especially in the primers as we marched in line here or there; 'Po kare kare ana', not especially suitable for marching, is the only one I can clearly remember. At high school, we sang songs in assembly; there seems to be still in my mind an echo of 'Men of Harlech', 'And did those feet in ancient time' and 'O Shenandoah, I hear you calling'. Such fragments, like the railway line and the dairy factory, pointed out and away.

There were books in the house other than the big history volumes I pored over – my father's liberal and radical classics such as Ruskin's *Unto This Last* and Bellamy's *Looking Backward* and the leather-bound prizes my uncle had won at Truro Cathedral School. These included the works of Shakespeare and the poems of Milton; I also seem to remember the name of Byron on an elegant red-leather spine. But that is as far as it went; I doubt if I ever opened any of them. Years later, in Dannevirke, a Methodist minister offended my better-educated mother by pointing to the bookshelf and saying 'I like to see some books about the house.' I suspect that being patronised in this way deepened her resolve to return to what was always for her *the* church.

But the minister, a jovial soul who liked to encourage suspicions of a misspent youth by demonstrating his skill at billiards, was in a way quite right. We were a people of the book and of the word: we read and read, steadily if not discriminatingly, through the nights and the years. It is evident from the notes in his exercise books that my father had read a good deal of socialist theory and economic writings – if he had not read Marx (and who could blame him for that?) he had read about him, perhaps in G. D. H. Cole's *What Marx Really Meant*, and in the pink volumes of the Left Book Club. When I was at Oxford my father asked me to tell Cole, then my supervisor, that he had helped Labour to win in 1935; I did, to Cole's slightly supercilious surprise. From this richly indiscriminate fare, I recall only a few items – a handful of the Richmal Crompton 'William' books (since denounced, to my astonishment and disbelief, as crypto-fascist in tendency), Tarzan books (since held to be racist), what my father called 'blood and thunder' books by Raphael Sabatini (piracy on the high seas), and P. C. Wren (blood and sand in the Foreign Legion), and later, from a lending library in Dannevirke, sensationalist exposés of a current affairs kind, with titles like 'I was Hitler's aunt/nurse/mistress/butler'.

Music, apart from hymns, was uncommon – oddly enough, in the light of my uncle's ability on the piano (after his death, bound volumes of Beethoven's sonatas turned up). It was not until I was at high school in the early 1940s that I heard a piece of 'real' music, something from Rimsky-Korsakov's *The Golden Cockerel*. I was electrified. We had music classes at high school for a time, until I became too busy with 'real' subjects. Usefully enough, I learned the names and voices of the instruments in the orchestra. The teacher's favourite test was 'Describe a trombone without using your hands'; I still cannot do so. Nor did the visual arts amount to much. Hanging on the wall at Makino Road there were two wild scenes of storms on the rocky Cornish coast, showing the Longships and the Lizard lighthouses. Nothing – apart from drawing vases in pencil with appropriate shading – was happening at school. This was the time, the 1930s, when an effort was being made to take the arts into schools, but it did not reach Feilding and Dannevirke.

Literature, and especially poetry, was closer to home. My mother treasured a poem I wrote about the sadness of leaving primary school, but she did not see another, of a vaguely Pre-Raphaelite kind, in which a young woman rather demurely took off her clothes. I think it had little to do with sex except in the most refined of ways. I was too busy and, mostly, too content to be much concerned with such matters, apart from noticing that the female body was, in a rather mysterious way, differently constructed. There is, too, in my memory and I trust nowhere else, a piece of bush mysticism inspired by reading a long quotation from Monte Holcroft in a *Listener* review of one of his essays.

At secondary school poetry was to be found in two remarkable books designed to teach other aspects of 'English', with bits of verse to illustrate matters of grammar and usage. What a wonderful subject it used to be –

everything from the split infinitive to the dramatic monologue! One was a slim work of local origin, *Our Living Language*, by Margaret Johnston with, I think, her own skilful light verse demonstrating such matters as 'loan words' and abbreviation. The other was by one Ogilvie, a grammar and much more, with sections on prosody and an exhaustive treatment of figures of speech. Alliteration was illustrated by Swinburne (who else?): 'Sounds of woods at sundown stirred / Welling water's winsome word'. Even then I suspected that this was going a bit far. As well, I did a bit of fossicking for myself, especially in the Dannevirke Public Library, where I was a regular reader of the *Bulletin*, and especially of the Red Page. And my father had a copy of Henry Holland's poems, *Red Roses on the Highways*, and used to quote from the one beginning 'When I am dead'.

In the sixth form poetry came alive, thanks to two remarkable teachers, one of French and the other of English. Miss Mahoney and Miss Trapp, as to their faces they were invariably addressed, were splendid examples of those generations of single women who made school teaching a life work. At another time they might have been academics, and both had strong connections with Victoria College. Perhaps such teachers were not commonly to be found in small country high schools; perhaps it was simply my good fortune to go to a school of some 400 pupils (the term 'student' was in those days reserved for higher levels) where, in everything from trade training to history and literature with sport most definitely included (as long as it was football), a high performance was both expected and nurtured.

Miss Mahoney was a Dublin Irishwoman, from a Catholic family which supported the British ascendancy. She had had the benefit of a Belgian convent education and knew France well. She was senior mistress, as I think the position was then called, and was reputed, inevitably and almost certainly libellously, to use her position to favour girls who shared her faith. Neither a girl nor a Catholic myself, I was a major recipient of her assistance. We had a rather boring text, *Tour de France en Auto*, in which a family observed and discussed the features and history of the places they travelled to – but not, as far as I can recall, the wine or the cuisine. But if it was boring, Miss Mahoney was not; she had been to these places and could easily be diverted into much more lively reminiscence. That was pleasanter than trying to read this strange tongue out loud and translate it into faltering English – and, I feel reasonably sure, more of an education.

In the upper sixth I took French as a university scholarship subject. One night a week I went to Miss Mahoney's flat for extra tuition. Chiefly she read her favourite poets, Baudelaire, Verlaine and Hérédia. Today I can still recall the erotic frisson that her translation of one poem – about a woman dancing and her body seen naked through the veils – gave me. That year, or perhaps the next when I took French I at Victoria College, I made my only attempt at translation, turning the opening stanza of a poem by Hérédia into English verse and not too badly, I thought at the time.

Miss Mahoney was plump, round-faced and wore her grey hair in a bun. Miss Trapp was thin, angular, tall and bent, an inveterate smoker with the makings in the sleeve of her gown and a hacking cough. (In later life, when she was a School Publications editor, I wrote a bulletin on New Zealand poetry for her.) I became a librarian, probably in the lower sixth, and processed the books she chose for the library. One was a slim selection of the poems of T. S. Eliot. She urged me to have a look at it. I did, with some puzzlement (as well as some obscure stirrings at the image of the girl with the hyacinths). I took it back with the comment that I found it very difficult. 'So do I,' she replied, 'but if you stay with it you will find it grows upon you.' I did, and it did. That remark is easily the most profound educational advice I have ever received. We also used a small green anthology of modern verse, which included both the traditional and the innovative. Through this, I made my first acquaintance with Yeats – 'Tread softly because you tread on my dreams' – and Stephen Spender's 'The Pylons' – 'Where often clouds shall lean their swan-white neck'. Of course, we read a good deal of other poetry under her guidance; Keats and Browning were the set texts for scholarship and I soon had Keats's odes by heart and, for the most part, they are still there. Browning gave me my first glimpse of the Italian Renaissance – 'Fra Lippo Lippi', 'The Bishop Orders his Tomb', 'My Last Duchess'. To my great delight there was a question in the scholarship examination which could be answered by writing on Eliot. I murdered it, concluding by quoting at some length from 'A Song for

Simeon'. Altogether, four years at Dannevirke High enabled me to leave with a feeling that I could manage most things of an academic kind, as long as it was a matter of words and not of numbers.

The lines of interest and enthusiasm that led into historical work have left equally clear traces – my father's talk of humanity's progress and my mother's remembrance of her local past, my Cornish connections, the history of the world in many volumes, *Our Nation's Story*, and the high excitement of the politics around me. I knew that 1935 was a turning point, that Spain, Abyssinia and the Anschluss mattered immensely, and that Neville Chamberlain's broadcast in 1939 – 'once again in the lives of most of us we are at war with Germany' – marked a momentous change.

There were no equivalents to the formidable Miss Mahoney and Miss Trapp teaching history at Dannevirke High School, but there were some sound practitioners; one of them, I discovered later, had written a good thesis on Scandinavian settlement of the district. The locality itself was a new lesson in history, a further reminder of a recent past and a distant but customary place. The town, the district and the school abounded with Danish and Norwegian proper names; Hansens and Rasmussens were plentiful. The very name 'Dannevirke' brought into the present the Prussian–Danish war of 1864, Schleswig-Holstein, Bismarck, the unification of Germany and the rise of nationalities; the Danish defences (the Danevirk) figured on the borough coat of arms. At school we studied nothing but European history; far from being a history which distanced me from my environment, it helped me to understand it. Are we now, as it has become modish to suppose, separated from that commodious past and should pay attention only to the meagre history of a small country stripped of those limitless resonances? If so, we impoverish ourselves; more, we mutilate, by a kind of amputation, the past of our own familiar soil.

The early 1940s were years of war; Europe and Asia were powerfully present. My father was guarding aerodromes against the Japanese peril; closer to the edge, my brother was on duty off Guadalcanal. The 'shorts' at the regularly attended matinees were full of war. Faced with the prospect of invasion, the Home Guard drilled with broomsticks and fireworks. I was a messenger under the Emergency Precautions Scheme and carried important information on a bicycle; on patriotic occasions I paraded down High Street with the school cadets. The National Film Unit tried to reassure us by panning a camera down a long line of planes – but we knew they were all trainers and transports. I dug an air raid shelter in the vegetable garden; it collapsed and my father was not pleased to have to re-dig and re-roof it. 'Always to islanders danger / Is what comes over the sea' – I did not then know Allen Curnow's poem (written about this time) but that was what we felt when Singapore fell to the Japanese and the British warships were sunk after their long journey from the North Sea.

While much of this was going on, we listened to the headmaster, E. N. Hogben, taking the sixth form for weekly sessions on current affairs. He led discussions exuberantly, and had us convinced that Europe was on the edge of an allied invasion long before it happened. But, in spite of the war, these were essentially years of work and achievement. The upper sixth had only five people in it – and the pace was too hot for one who dropped out and went back to the farm. We did not get much supervision and worked away in a small room set aside for us; once, when I was strolling in the school grounds, I was accosted by 'the Head' who merely remarked, 'You and I, Oliver, seem to be the only ones with nothing to do.' I went back to work, possibly to continue my reading of H. A. L. Fisher's *History of Europe*, an excellent piece of prose, in no way a textbook but an eloquent and sceptical overview of a history which I took to be my own. Better to read, I later realised, a good book which was wrong here and there than a careful textbook that never ran the risk.

At the end of the upper sixth year, with the war still far from over, we sat the scholarship examination; for reasons which may have had something to do with my lack of Latin and probably more with the limitations of the curriculum, I had to take mathematics and chemistry, at which I was incompetent, as well as English and history, at which I excelled, and French, which I could at least manage. As a result, my marks were distributed along a range from the 20s to the 80s. Enough in aggregate for a bursary, but not for a scholarship. Still, with savings over the years from Saturday work at the butcher's shop and with the money I would earn from summer work, the bursary was sufficient to take me to Victoria University College in 1943.

But first, with two friends (one of whom came from a family so anti-Catholic that the father would not allow his initials to appear in the phone book but insisted upon 'Robt. C.'), I went north to Hastings, to work in the Tomoana freezing works, where my informal education continued steadily. While we waited for the killing season to open, we looked for work in the market gardens. It was the time for pea-picking and we were given a lift from the office, where we asked for work, to the pea fields in a large car driven by a dumpy but authoritative figure – James Wattie, we soon realised, himself. On the fields we worked individually; Maori, we noticed, worked communally – old ladies with furious fingers sat on upturned boxes and stripped the vines a mob of small children brought to them.

I did not fully realise it at the time, but three successive seasons spent in Hastings provided my first lessons in what we did not yet call biculturalism. Maori, it will have become clear, did not figure largely in my upbringing. At Feilding Ag, I knew two members of the Te Punga family, but the elder was a lofty senior boy and the younger, nearer my own age, a bit of a bully from whom one kept a respectful distance. The Durie family, whose members Eddie and Mason I was to meet much later, were quite unknown to me, even though I spent holidays at Taonui, close to their home. The gap was social as well as ethnic; they were farming gentry, we were labouring folk. At Dannevirke I had a close friend who was one of the Paewai family; we swam together in the town baths early in the morning, training for the school sports. This was the only sport I was at all good at, but he was in a class of his own. He died from (I think) falling off the tray of a truck; I was shocked that such speed and beauty and skill should end so abruptly. I was also friendly with Sam Mihaere, later a Maori welfare officer and the top-polling Palmerston North city councillor, not at all athletic because he was a polio victim but determined to get on. He took Maori for university entrance (but there was no teaching for him at school) and said that it was a difficult language.

In the Tomoana freezing works at Hastings, Maori were numerous. We were employed on the killing floor as odd-job hands; by falsifying our ages we received full wages and I still recall my first envelope containing £6 19*s* 2*d* for the week. Each floor had a shower room and a lunch room; we went, however, to the floor below, where the offal and other bits came down the chutes and were processed. Maybe there was a bit of unofficial segregation; the room we chose had many more Maori than the one above and we felt that we had ended up in the better place. There was a young man who picked up the book I was reading with my lunch, Bacon's *Essays*, perhaps a set book for English the following year. Yes, he had read it at school (Te Aute, probably) but he was not going on with education. That seemed fair enough at the time. And, imposingly, there was a large man who effortlessly dominated the table and indeed the room. He was good to the three Pakeha boys, not at all condescendingly but with a warm acceptance. I gathered that he was an important leader; here he was a freezing worker, out there he was a man of rank. This impressed upon me for the first time that there was another society to be taken into account; in time I would add to this awareness a realisation that there was another history.

But the presence of the European past was also reinforced, and not only by the carcasses we sent down to the freezing chambers on their way, like the butter from the Makino factory, to a distant market, but also by a handful of older men I came to know quite well. A tiny Scot worked on the cooling floor, where we were often sent; he had a lovely accent and quoted bits of verse at us, probably from Burns. Two others made a greater impact. We wore wooden clogs with a horseshoe-like steel strip around the rim; these strips wore out on the concrete floors and the clogs had to be taken upstairs to a loft where an eloquent Irishman repaired them. Sharing that upstairs space was an engineer, Tom Hanlon, an intellectual who was studying externally from Victoria, especially philosophy. Years later I went with him to the Wellington Town Hall for his graduation, and then lost contact. He and the shoemaker were often locked in ideological combat, Tom advancing the affirmations of the Enlightenment and the Irishman, a firm Catholic, denouncing the Greek 'cult of the body beautiful'. The connection between the two now escapes me, but it seemed right enough at the time. At the end of the 1942–43 killing season I left for Wellington and Victoria College.

CHAPTER FIVE

A Time of Opening

When I set off for the new world in 1943, I had £90 in my Post Office Savings Bank account – £30 from my bursary, £30 saved over the years and £30 earned at the freezing works during the summer – and this was enough to see me through the year. The new world, however, was not especially new until my second year. In the first I lived with a retired Cornish couple, an honorary aunt and uncle, in a small house in Newtown, at the end of a cul-de-sac and backing on the green belt. My 'uncle', a tiny, squat man with a broad face, had, I think, been in the building trade, perhaps driving a cart; he still spoke with an accent. My 'aunt' was noticeably more genteel (Cornish males seem always to have married upwards), lacked an accent and had some claim to an earlier connection with the household of Lord Galway, a recent Governor-General – a domestic servant, we spitefully supposed, but she received the occasional invitation to Government House.

It was a circumscribed life, as domestic as it had been in Dannevirke and without much to distinguish the suburb from the small town. Each day I took the tram to the city and climbed the hill to the college; sometimes I cheated on the tram fare for some extra spending money. I had taken my bike to Wellington but after a few trips trundling it up The Terrace and Salamanca Road I left it behind. Each night I returned to my evening meal, to some more work and to my night's sleep. I once heard loud cries coming from the town belt, but stayed fearfully in my bed, the safe suburb too suddenly juxtaposed with the unsafe wild.

Already I had begun to collect books; Smith's on Mercer Street had more to offer than the slim pickings of the Dannevirke second-hand shop. I bought a two-volume collected edition of Swinburne; I had somehow become curious about *fin de siècle* decadence. But I did not get through much of it; the celebrated eroticism and irreligion already seemed a bit tame. For that matter, my own sexuality was also a bit tame and remained so for altogether too long. This was not a time for new departures, nor was it for many years.

I was more adventurous in religion, however, and through the leader of the Bible class at the local Methodist church, Wilf Layton, a pacifist, I was drawn to the strength of that position. The crunch point came a year or so later, when I approached the age at which I would be called up. I had an awkward exchange with each of my parents. My mother pointedly recalled her brother's death in the first war. I talked with my father in the garden he had made at the Air Force station at Milson; with his example in front of me, I said, I could not become a conscientious objector. Family loyalty won the day over my inner inclination – but maybe I simply could not contemplate the upset that conscientious objection would entail. When the call-up came, I reported to the Dannevirke drill hall, was peered at and into, and pronounced fit for service. Then the war saved me from the consequences of this half-hearted decision by coming to an end.

My first year university course provided few, if any, challenges; indeed, it was less exciting intellectually than the upper sixth at Dannevirke High. We were far removed from our lecturers; if there were people around as stimulating as my two admirable sixth form teachers, they were too distant for me to benefit. Is it possible to spend a year listening to those great men, Fred Wood and John Beaglehole, and not remember a word or a thought? It is, and it is possible to remember of Ian Gordon only his first lecture, spent organising the English I tutorial programme. Literature survived his ministrations, as it did those of Bruce Cochran, more celebrated for a little book on sexual relationships. Ernest Beaglehole delivered psychology lectures which seemed to be one long sentence without punctuation. (It was a malicious rumour that he ended the lecture precisely when the clock struck, whether in mid-sentence or not.)

The professor of French, Boyd-Wilson, did impress, but not with his scholarship. He began the year by telling a class of fifty or so that we were too many for his liking and he counted upon our being fewer by the end of the first term. I thought this an arrogant approach; most of those in the class were, like me, only there because at that time a foreign language was compulsory. But perhaps he was provoking us to greater effort? It had that result in my case; I worked so hard (at an activity I found deeply uncongenial) that I ended up with rather more than the scratch pass I needed and reflected dourly upon the saying that every mark over 50 was one wasted. There was, however, some slight gain; Loti's *Pêcheur d'Islande* has still a lingering flavour, but *Half-hours with Modern French Authors* (I think it was called) has not.

My later conviction that you do not need the language to benefit from another culture may have been, in part, prompted by this experience, but it owed more to the one course in those otherwise humdrum years which really opened my mind, Greek HAL (history, art and literature), taught by two dry-as-dust pedants, John Rankine Brown and L. H. G. Greenwood. Rankine Browne was big and burly, with a bristling moustache through which he (unintentionally but liberally) sprayed the front row, which we avoided. Greenwood was a tiny wispy figure of a man with a shy and retiring disposition, painfully obvious in his lectures. He was said to have been marooned in New Zealand by the war. Neither was a crowd pleaser; nor, this being a throwaway course for those lacking Latin and Greek, was it especially exacting.

But, thanks to these venerable scholars, a new civilisation entered my world, a new continent to enlarge an old map, a marvellous territory for an avid imagination to annex. Probably, too, this experience bred in me a deep respect for mere unadorned learning. Greek history was a vast and highly informative set text by J. B. Bury; art was reproductions of statues and vase paintings and the ground plans of temples projected on a screen; literature was a romantic translation of Aristophanes' *The Frogs* and a shamelessly rhetorical translation of the *Iliad*. The course has remained in my mind as (without disrespect, or without much of it, to the other courses) the most awakening experience of my BA years.

I survived English to the end of my second year but, as I found that the unavoidable language paper came close to sinking the whole unit, did not go on to English III. Old and Middle English, like Latin and French earlier and Maori much later, I found to be simply beyond my capacity – not that the teaching, in the hands of Bruce Cochran and a patently bored Jim Bertram, helped any. Though English was not in itself an enlightening experience, one of the set texts did prove in the long run a significant point of departure, Newman's *Idea of a University*. Later Ian Gordon said that he had chosen it to instil some idea of what university should be like. I doubt if it had that effect upon a ragtag and bobtail first-year class which included a large contingent of commerce degree conscripts. But it led me, a few years later, to Newman's *Apologia*, and thence to my love affair with the Oxford Movement and beyond that, with a logic which I tried for some time to resist, to what Anglo-Catholics used to refer to as 'the post-Tridentine papal communion'.

Eventually, Oxford itself completed the process that reading about Oxford had begun; there I was confirmed and attached myself to the High Church end of the Anglican spectrum even though, in some degree for the sake of marital accord, I attended the middle-of-the-road observances of St Mary's, the university church where Newman had preached his great sermons. Though that shift, in its turn, led elsewhere, I retain a keen appreciation and a slightly perplexed respect for the deep-rootedness and effortless assurance of Anglicanism on its home ground, at least as I experienced it in the 1950s. There is a stone wall in Littlemore surrounding the house in which Newman agonised before going over to Rome; it bears a plaque with the limpid inscription 'Here lived John Henry Newman, Vicar of St Mary's, later Cardinal.' The cheek, the sheer Anglican cheek!

After an initial period of marking time, life at Victoria began to open up – more outside the lecture room than in it. I have come to believe that one of the really important things a university can do is to encourage an environment in which people may educate each other – some of them will be official teachers but many, perhaps most, will be other students. In 1944 I went to live at Weir House, a university hostel at that time exclusively for males. Here my interest in literature, history and religion as intellectual activities flourished. I became sporadically active in the college Debating Society and on the student paper *Salient*, where I wrote from time to time on the relationship between literature and politics – then a much-discussed topic thanks to the vogue of socialist realism. Though I no longer went to church or Bible class, I began attending Student Christian Movement meetings at which a wide range of topics was discussed – politics, literature, philosophy as well as (but not too often) religion.

At Weir House I shared a room with Bill Mabbett, also from Dannevirke High School, one of the very few taking German for his BA major. He insisted upon his peasant origins – and occasionally wrote poems about them (one told of the mud squeezed between his bare toes). He chose to counter the modish leftism of the times with a poster of Mussolini on the wall of our room, which became something of a literary cell and the centre of a tiny literary explosion. Here the *Weir House Magazine*, an inconspicuous annual, was edited and became a vehicle for a few poems as well as the customary notes and jokes. People who had never dreamed of doing so wrote a poem or two and returned to silence as abruptly as they had emerged from it. The future public servant and consultant, Geoffrey Datson, surprised himself by coming third in the poetry competition run by the student annual, *The Spike*. (A few years back I read that poem at his funeral service in Old St Paul's.) Basil Dowling, then at Library School, was the judge; he placed me first and Pat Wilson second. Literature, for a time, became fashionable. The house was divided between two factions, designated not 'aesthetes' and 'athletes' but, schoolboyishly enough, 'good chaps' and 'fine sports'. Jejune as it must now seem, these labels were worn proudly, if ironically, by a number of people later to become distinguished in the service of church and state, science and literature.

There were two at Weir House, however, for whom poetry was not a passing fancy but a lifelong passion, Pat Wilson and Alistair Campbell. I would not place myself alongside them as a poet, but for a time we did a good deal together, although they were closer to each other than I was to either. Pat was writing constantly and a few of these poems went into his first volume, *The Bright Sea*. At the time I did not recognise the virtue of his restraint, his distaste for rhetoric and his avoidance of any but the most understated of gestures. Oddly, perhaps, this did not lessen Pat's enthusiasm for Alistair Campbell's exuberantly rhetorical lyrics; he was at that time writing the love poems which appeared in *Mine Eyes Dazzle*. Pat once told how Alistair would come to his room time and time again and exclaim 'I've written another one!' For my own part, I discovered a capacity for pastiche and parody which could have led me into light verse but, except once in a while, did not. Considerably influenced by Wordsworth's *Prelude*, I worked in a romantic mode and, as tramping extended my horizons in the later 1940s, took from landscape a set of images to express (and, as surely, conceal) my inner hopes and fears. Much later, the more decorous of these were published in *Fire Without Phoenix*. Sometimes it seems to me that I have been looking for the phoenix ever since.

This shared excitement helped to generate a burst of writing and publication which has come to occupy a small place in literary history. Two short-lived periodicals were its main manifestations: *Hilltop*, for which John Thomson, a Nelson College friend of Pat's, was the guiding spirit, and its successor *Arachne*, into which it was transformed by Erik Schwimmer. At the time all this seemed more like a mix of good fun and self-discovery than a serious literary enterprise – but that, it may be, is how literary movements begin. The story of the 'Wellington poets' of the 1940s has been elaborated into a broader 'Wellington school' (including Louis Johnson, Erik Schwimmer, Hubert Witheford and James Baxter) defining itself in opposition to an equally improbable 'Auckland school'. Fair enough: it is the habit (and the right) of the present to impose its shape on the past, but in this past I can see only a few people wrestling with the word and winning now and then. That was exciting enough. It was exciting, too, to find a way into print and so lay a hesitant claim to a place, maybe just the beginning of a place, in the long history of words set down on a page in the hope that they would last.

We were, for the most part, also winning academically. None of us was in danger of cultivating the kind of university non-career which Baxter was pursuing at the same time in Otago and Canterbury, or the bohemian marginality of Johnson, on a life-support system contemptuously accepted from journalism. Alistair devoted himself to Latin, with notable success under the guidance of Rankine Brown's successor, the learned H. A. Murray. His expertise in Latin was more evident then than his Polynesian origins. Alistair did not become an academic but, after odd-jobbing in his beloved Central Otago, finished his degree and found a long-term haven in the School Publications Branch of the Department of Education.

Pat Wilson completed – I still wonder why – two MAs, in philosophy and education, and went on to write a PhD thesis on William Blake. (According to a later and possibly untrue tale, the departments of philosophy and English tossed his thesis to and fro, each saying 'It's yours, not ours.') In his bed-sit overlooking Oriental Bay, Pat papered the walls with the complete works of Blake, using up two copies of the Nonesuch edition, and walked around the room making correlations and comparisons. That done, he departed for England to study music and music teaching, married and had children, published poems in Britain for a brief period, lived in a London suburb and brought out a final book – a rather bleak and even angry one – in New Zealand not long before his death. Before that time we had become strangers and I did not see him on his few return visits to New Zealand. That still saddens me.

For my part, manpowered in the last year of the war and preserving my academic career by finding an 'essential' job in the public service, I became a part-time student. A year taking only political science allowed me plenty of time for more literary endeavours. I am glad that it was the year for the history of political theory, for that gave me another thick book to absorb, the text by Sabine, not a work of deep analysis but a source of much information. I had a further year taking only History III and this was a chancier venture: in one of the three final examinations we were told to choose four questions; there were just four I could manage and the rest I could hardly recognise. My luck held and I did well enough to prompt my brother to help me through a full-time honours year. His generosity enabled me to take a long step towards becoming an historian; for this my gratitude knows no bounds.

Some of us needed to make a few social adjustments, obligatory in those starchy days if one wished to join the ranks of the discerning and the well-informed. Coffee was a socio-intellectual marker and had to be drunk black and unsweetened, fairly regularly in the French Maid cafe on Lambton Quay near Stewart Dawson's corner. The use of alcohol was, for a child of an abstinent family, an initiation undergone with mixed feelings of curiosity and guilt; it was many years before I could enter a pub without a slight sense of daring. I did not embark upon my drawn battle with whisky at this stage, but wine was there to be accommodated; I made my peace with dry sherry (Springbok, in those peaceful pre-anti-apartheid days), though agreeing with Bill Mabbett's verdict, upon a first acquaintance, that it tasted like rather bitter dishwater. Beer, however, was still the unchallenged king — beer carried into Weir House in crates during its wardenless days, draught beer in the packed pubs of the dying years of six o'clock closing (often with lexicographer Harry Orsman's reel-to-reel recorder spinning under the bar), beer vastly consumed by the phenomenal Baxter after his migration north, beer home-brewed in the beat-up rented cottage I lived in for a time behind the Western Park hotel and often consumed by the poet on the way to his Karori mail run.

Many years later, living in Palmerston North, I celebrated these distant times by writing a short series of unrhymed sonnets, entitled simply 'Portraits', each addressed to a friend. To Alistair and Pat I added Jim Baxter, Charles Brasch, Louis Johnson and Erik Schwimmer, for they were important to me at that time and in the future. I wanted to celebrate the good fortune of being in their company when I first learned that words, if they did not quite earn you a living, at least gave you a life. Books had been my familiar companions from my earliest years; now I discovered that it was possible to knock, even hesitantly, upon the door which opened upon that capacious world.

In childhood I had learned something of the power of the word and the range of its uses. Now my realisation of its centrality to literature, politics, religion and history — all familiar to me for as long as I could look back — grew deeper in a richer soil. No one of these manifestations of the authority and power of the word has ever quite left me, although over the years some have grown and others waned. Around the same time my awareness expanded to include those activities so neglected in my early years, music and the visual arts; they, too, have become ingrained in my everyday living and thinking. The impact of the wartime émigré Jewish community was crucial, especially the Schwimmer family, whose Wadestown house (I suspect to the annoyance of the father, Felix) became a centre for parties and talk. Erik, much more sophisticated than any of us and with an exotic past in the Dutch East Indies (then so-called) and in literary circles in Australia (he was present at the birth of the Ern Malley hoax), tried to introduce us to existentialism – and, indeed, I did read Camus, to my great advantage.

Music, all kinds of it, I absorbed in undiscriminating gulps. Neil Mountier, a close friend of Pat's, had an extensive collection of jazz and swing on 10-inch 78s. Pat Wilson and Gib Bogle were fine performers on the piano of the kind of jazz called 'boogie'. I added the great names of early jazz and blues to my expanding pantheon – Louis Armstrong, Fats Waller, Bessie Smith and Duke Ellington. It did not seem incongruous to be acquiring a taste for classical music at the same time. The first recording I bought was a second-hand and very scratchy *Scheherazade* on 12-inch 78s, to what end I will never know, for I did not possess a record player. The only remark worth making about adding the names of, say, Beethoven, Schubert, Schumann and Brahms to my ever-extending list is that only a few years before they were as unknown to me as the heroes of jazz. Music, of a kind, was part of my job in the Broadcasting Service, to which I had migrated from Internal Affairs. I had to sort out enough 78s for Lunch Music and Dinner Music – the latter programme supposed to be fairly light and fluffy. Snobbishly perhaps, I filled it up with short classical pieces and movements from larger works, until I was told to stop.

In the later 1940s I heard this music performed live for the first time. The concerts provided by the newly formed Chamber Music Society, the post-war visits of Lili Kraus, Solomon, Ninon Vallin and the Boyd Neel String Orchestra, the Room 6 concerts at Victoria College organised by Fred Page – firmly fixed in my memory by Maurice Clare playing the Beethoven violin sonatas and Joan Wood singing, perhaps, Schubert –

opened new realms. Soon after his arrival in Wellington, a stranger turned up to a meeting of the college Poetry Society (it was affiliated in order to secure a subsidy) held in a Weir House room to discuss New Zealand poetry, something we were in the process of discovering (with the help of illicitly borrowed copies from the Turnbull Library). It was Douglas Lilburn, who knew most of the people we were finding out about; his dour and dedicated personality was in itself an enlightenment. Some of us, especially Alistair and Pat though I went along quite often, became visitors to his flat on The Terrace and later to his storm-threatened cottage at Paekakariki.

The visual arts, also no part of my inheritance, became familiar through people who painted and drew – Hank Schwimmer in a little cellar room off Bolton Street, Theo Schoon observed on Wellington streets in a toga, Douglas McDiarmid, a friend of John Thomson's, and Sam Cairncross of whom Louis Johnson told barely credible tales. And once, though we had little to say to each other, I met Toss Woollaston when I was baby-sitting for the Pages. There were galleries and exhibitions of paintings by people who actually lived and worked close by or not far off – at the French Maid (Cairncross and the delicate drawings of Barc), at the Architectural Centre and at the Wellington Public Library. Here the early religious paintings of Colin McCahon were exhibited; their enormous impact upon me (intensified by a residual but nagging religious bent) was not in the least diminished by John Beaglehole's hostile (and perplexed?) review in *Landfall*. Around the same time I came to know McCahon's great Otago Peninsula landscape hanging on Mario and Hilda Fleischl's wall, a painting they had commissioned.

It was an exciting new world and a manageably compact one; the specialisation of interests and activity had not yet set in. Literature, music, theatre, the visual arts and the life of the mind were all the business of a fairly homogeneous body of practitioners, consumers and supporters – a small and in some ways embattled and self-conscious intelligentsia (perhaps Coleridge's term 'clerisy' would be closer) into whose ranks the newcomer was welcomed. But writing remained at the centre of my life and rapidly became an expanding centre. Charles Brasch, founder of the quarterly *Landfall* and an editor who took literature as a force for social salvation (a humanist heresy which the residues of traditional religion saved me from), travelled the country in a quasi-episcopal manner, inquiring, encouraging and sometimes reproving. He was often in Wellington, and became an admired and loved friend. The little magazines coming out of Wellington were all very well in their way, but it was obvious that publication in *Landfall* would signify arrival on the wider stage. That happened to me in 1948, when Charles published my 'Death and the Maiden'. While I was the first of the group to receive that accolade, Pat and Alistair published their books well before I did; Alistair's *Mine Eyes Dazzle* was a runaway success.

Poetry competed (in the end unsuccessfully) with my two other interests – politics and history. I enjoyed the carry-on of student politics and found myself unable – an inability that lasted for years – to keep away from protest and agitation. My first attempt to participate in one of the regular debates run by the Debating Society, in those days a power in the college, ended in discomfiture. The motion was 'That Russia is the hope of civilisation'; after the German invasion of Russia that proposition had become more plausible. I intended to speak in favour of the motion, coming up from the floor to the stage for the first time, an unnerving experience. I have no notion of what I said, but it prompted a well-known and fierce left-wing woman to denounce me as 'a lily-white Caucasian'. Ever since, and not only because of that episode, I have been wary of slanging matches; invariably I find myself misrepresented, usually through my own fault, and too often I lose both my temper and the argument.

The ending of the war, first in Europe and then in the Pacific, ushered in a brief Indian summer before the cold war took hold. Films were screened showing the opening of the death camps and the devastation at Hiroshima and Nagasaki, but those tragedies were eclipsed by euphoria at the war's end. There was dancing in the streets of Wellington and women drinking in public bars; on Lambton Quay an elderly Chinese man walked solemnly into the middle of the street, lit an immense firework and regarded it expressionlessly before he went back to his shop. There were Christmas cards bearing the linked images of Churchill, Stalin and Roosevelt; I blush to recount it, but I bought one in a Dannevirke bookshop and sent it to a Communist friend in Wellington, inscribed 'And now abide these three, Britain, America and Russia, and the greatest of these is Russia.' He had tried to recruit me into the party, saying that I could become a 'second Palme Dutt' – a person of whom I had not heard at that time. How he responded (if he did at all) to my evocation of St Paul I do not remember.

At Weir House, as well as poets, there were people who would become parsons and preachers – a couple of professors of religious studies, a moderator, a bishop – and troublesome laymen. Peter McKenzie, Albert Moore, Denzil Brown, Godfrey Wilson, Erle Robinson and Harold Gilmore did more than keep my interest in religion alive; they helped to stiffen it with some intellectual muscle. There were late-night discussions over coffee, continuing in the communal showers for as long as the hot water lasted. I realised that conviction and belief came more readily to most of these people than to me; I have never been able to avoid observing myself quizzically and saying 'Yes – well, perhaps.' But that absence of firm commitment was not uncommon in the Student Christian Movement, whose meetings and conferences I attended for a time during the middle 1940s.

These meetings were usually held in the houses of well-to-do supporters and sometimes in the delightful surroundings of Wallis House, a conference centre in the Hutt valley. There I was deeply impressed by a quiet Quaker, Edward Dowsett, talking simply and movingly about pacifism – even though my earlier interest had waned, and I found it impossible to bridge the gap between the logic of the pacifist case and its impracticality. Another meeting, suitably held in a substantial Karori house, was addressed by the youngish Presbyterian lawyer, politician and future National Prime Minister, Jack Marshall. Harry Evison (not a regular SCM participant by any means) gave him a hard time at the end. 'You sound like a Communist,' Marshall said. 'I am a Communist,' replied Evison to the evident astonishment of the speaker.

At an SCM conference in Dunedin I first came to know Donald Anderson, severely disabled by cerebral palsy, from whom I (like many others) learned a good deal about courage and humility. I saw more of him in Oxford a few years later, when he was reading English at Magdalen College. He was a frequent visitor to the semi-detached house my wife and

I and a small first son, John Benedict, occupied in a drab outlying housing estate. With a slight over-insistence on his capacity to do everyday things, he would dry the dishes and stack them into perilous piles. He enjoyed being mistaken for a drunk when he was offered assistance in crossing a road, and I once saw him riding a large tricycle down the busy street next to his college, probably terrified and certainly terrifying the motorists in his trajectory. After completing his BLitt, teaching school in Birmingham, getting married and being appointed to a job teaching English at Palmerston North University College, he died of a heart attack – taking a rest among the graves and trees of St Mary's church in New Plymouth while travelling to meet extramural students.

The SCM, thanks to the breadth of the interests it provided a place for, was a major cultural as well as religious meeting ground, at least in this limited milieu. For a time, the dominant figure at Victoria was its chaplain, Martin G. Sullivan, and his wife, Doris. Both were essentially establishment people; he, it was reliably reported, was the *éminence grise* behind the unseating of the left-wing Student Association executive when it was rash enough to congratulate Klement Gottwald on the Communist coup d'état in Prague. Many years later, after Martin had become Dean of St Paul's in London, I called at the deanery while on leave. Walking down a passage from the door he paused before a large portrait of John Donne. 'One of my more illustrious predecessors,' he remarked, with a nonchalant gesture. I think the burden of the past, and for that matter of the present, rested rather lightly upon him.

For me the past started to become a passion towards the end of the 1940s and, prospectively at least, a profession. The honours course in history brought me close (for the first time) to Fred Wood and John Beaglehole, and to the lovable and exotic presence of Peter Munz. When I first knew Peter, in 1945 as an assistant lecturer, he was already celebrated for an MA thesis on the philosophy of history, reputed to consist of fifty-five pages of text and twice that number devoted to references. Now that he had returned from Cambridge I was often in his company and, through him, that of Hubert Witheford and John O'Shea, historians who took their history into poetry and film. Peter was the first historian I had encountered to whom ideas mattered more than anything else. I learned from him that there was a wide world of scholarship and intellect out there and that I might have a chance to knock upon that door as well.

For one of the honours papers, the student was to draw upon all the wisdom and insight that had been garnered during the year and write a long essay upon a broad historical topic. This examination provided my first entirely satisfying intellectual experience as I calmly and collectedly composed an essay on the relationship between nationalism and imperialism. I developed a paradox as I wrote – that the former was certain to evolve into the latter and so, as we would now put it, self-destruct by denyingits basic premise. Now, with a greater abundance of examples to hand, I can see the fallacy in the argument – one nationalism is not in the least weakened by bringing about the destruction of another. Quite the contrary, that is what it is for.

John Beaglehole took a class in historical method – not in the philosophy of history, for which he professed a profound contempt – in his long narrow attic room, filled with pipe smoke and not at all warmed by an ancient heater with a faintly glowing coil at the centre of a round copper reflector. I recall nothing more than Beaglehole picking up a matchbox and asking us to consider whether or not it could be classed as an archival record. (It is, I can now appreciate, a good question but I do not remember the answer.) I had read his *New Zealand: A Short History* and admired its intellectual brilliance; later I came to regret that he had not gone on to become the first major historian of New Zealand. This I discovered to be an unacceptable opinion among those who prefer a splendidly executed piece of eighteenth century English history to what could have been the foundation work in modern New Zealand history.

Fred Wood I loved as well as respected; more precisely, I began to do so in these years. I took his two honours courses, the compulsory one in British constitutional history and a special topic, 'The growth of philosophical radicalism'. In constitutional history I found a kind of history which, so it then seemed, admitted of no uncertainty – you either got it dead right or dead wrong. There was, too, the engaging if clumsy precision of legalistic language, awkward just because it was designed to get it right, a new variation on the power of the word. I now know, having been involved in the constitutional arguments prompted by the Waitangi Tribunal, that the words used in this kind of history are no more value-free than any other terminology, even though their users may score a point or two by pretending that they are. Nevertheless, the study gave me an enhanced respect for the virtues of verbal precision.

The intellectual turmoil of early nineteenth century Britain, as mediated through Halévy's great book on philosophical radicalism and Fred Wood's quizzical interrogation of seminar papers, helped me to a realisation of the way in which historical discourse becomes an obscurantist polemic if complexity is not both respected and brought under intellectual control. This, in its turn, has had its fruit in later labours: an ingrained hostility to such statements as 'The Treaty of Waitangi is a perfectly simple document', and 'The Treaty is so muddled that no reliable interpretation can be placed upon it.' A plague, in other words, upon all those who have not the patience and persistence to think historically. This, more than anything else, I learned from Fred Wood.

In 1952, the celebrated Hope Gibbons fire prompted a controversy by which, for a time, I entered into the folklore of New Zealand history. A whole section of the National (then Dominion) Archives was stored in this building in downtown Wellington and was destroyed by a fire which raged through it. A southerly whipped up the flames and carried, perhaps with a malignant irony, charred papers still bearing evidence of their provenance (Marine Department and so on faintly discernible) into Kelburn gardens, including that of the Woods. The lamentations of historians, those guardians of the archival heritage (not that that word had yet become fashionable), rose in remonstrance to the unregarding heavens. In response to a pious editorial, I wrote a brief letter to the *Listener* saying that, given the overproduction of such material and given the way in which fire, flood and other forms of destruction had over the centuries reduced the evidential deposit of the past to manageable proportions, this event might more properly be regarded as a help than a hindrance to future historians. Eric McCormick wrote a furious letter in reply, saying that while one expected the Goths and the Vandals to attack from the outside it was novel to find them within the citadel. Peter Munz contemplated a letter to the editor saying that McCormick was out of date: it had become accepted that the Goths were the preservers not the destroyers of civilisation. But I doubt if he sent it. Decades later, I put research students at Massey to work on early administrative history; they regularly met the phrase 'Lost in the Hope Gibbons fire' in response to their requests at National Archives. I remain unconvinced, however, that history has suffered.

After completing the papers for MA, I returned to my employment in the Broadcasting Service. One day, before results were out, I had a phone call from Fred asking if I would be interested in a junior lectureship in the following year. I replied, with some caution, that it seemed to me that I would not be wise to accept that offer unless my papers gave me a firm prospect of a first-class degree (I knew that one had not been awarded at Victoria for many years). With even greater caution he replied (and I can still hear him, so characteristic was the utterance) that he agreed completely with my assessment but that he could not possibly tell me. I gathered, later, that there was some to-ing and fro-ing with the assessor, William Morrell, as to whether I was heading for a high second or a low first. I took the risk, accepted the job and became, rubbing my eyes in surprise, an academic.

I wrote my thesis as a member of staff. I had become fascinated with seventeenth century English history (the possibility of doing a New Zealand research topic did not even occur to me). This was one of the fields in which Alexander Turnbull had been most assiduous as a collector. Through the good offices of Tony Murray-Oliver I had – it would be unthinkable today – free access to the shelves of the Turnbull Library. Here I chanced upon a sizeable, if not quite complete, collection of the pamphlets of Roger L'Estrange, active as an ardent royalist during the Restoration period and (to his eventual misfortune) beyond into the reign of James II and the 1688 revolution. So great is serendipity that I found in the General Assembly Library a full set of the newspaper L'Estrange had also produced.

What the argument of my thesis might have been I now forget. I remember, vividly, the pleasure of reading and note-taking long after closing time in the fine front room of what is now Turnbull House, surrounded by elegant glass-fronted bookcases filled with beautifully bound books.

Later I would find myself working in the Bodleian, but even the venerable Duke Humfrey's Library did not give me the same feeling of intimacy with a departed world. For my inevitably rushed closing chapter, I wrote the final copy direct from the sources on a portable typewriter (a gift from roving Uncle George). I do not think it did seventeenth century studies much good, but it did some for me; the thesis persuaded my assessor to give me the first without which I would have become a former academic.

It was still a close-run thing. Everything turned on winning a postgraduate scholarship – *the* postgraduate scholarship, for there was one each year for all arts graduates in the country. It was possible to apply in two successive years and on the first try I missed. The second time around I was staying with Peter and Anne Munz in a seaside bach when the results were due. We had no phone and I asked Peter if he would go to a nearby house and find out. He did, after some hesitation; he said he was afraid I would never speak to him again if he brought back bad news. But the news was good. I would, before long, set off on the last long stage of the return journey to my father's country and to an Oxford he had probably not heard of when he lived there, so remote would it have been from the life he left behind forty years earlier.

CHAPTER SIX

Departures and Journeys

Six or so weeks before leaving for Oxford in 1951, I embarked upon another kind of voyage, life as a married man. The early years of married life in Oxford were good – good for the two of us as husband and wife and, before the episode was over, as parents. The two departures went well together, give or take a few mishaps and misadventures along the way – or so it seems in retrospect. I had met Dorothy Rachel Nielsen about two years earlier at a Student Christian Movement conference in Christchurch; my first memory is that she was among the local members who prepared breakfast for those arriving by the early morning ferry from the north. Within a day or so I found myself drawn strongly to her.

She sang in the Christchurch Harmonic Society Choir and was later to join the Bach Choir in Oxford. She played the piano well; I recall Bach preludes and fugues in quantity and a Schubert impromptu in the ship's concert on the way to England. But she did not enjoy public performances. There was also a haunting Bach slow movement, which I can still hear, played over and over again many years later after a serious quarrel. She had been, briefly, to art school and I still have some skilful drawings. Her intellectual capacity was great; when she resumed her studies late in life, she took top grades in linguistics and religious studies, surprising herself but no one else.

Dorothy was remarkably beautiful – tall and slender and, from her Norwegian ancestry, blue-eyed with long straight fair hair and classically regular features – and she had a rare quality of stillness. Soon after we met she left Canterbury College, where she had been studying English and history, for nursing. For a time she trained in Wellington before returning to Christchurch. There I visited her regularly, travelling to and fro on Friday and Sunday nights on the ferry. At some point, during a long walk on Mt Kaukau near Wellington, we became, in an informal way, engaged. Deeply in love, I experienced for the first time the excitement and the distancing from the everyday world that goes with that risky condition.

Twice, before our marriage, she tried to put an end to the relationship. She said, quite simply, that it would be best for me if I went away, for she would bring too much trouble with her – by this time I knew enough of her childhood and difficult family situation to know what she meant. But in my arrogance and from a blind belief in my capacity to fix anything, I refused to be put off. We were married in June 1951 on a cold winter's day in Christchurch. I arrived at the church a little late (by tram, after the taxi failed to turn up at Harry Scott's flat where I was staying) to see my father doubled up with laughter at this characteristic behaviour. There was a stiff little party at my parents-in-law's house, with the two family cohorts huddling together in separate clumps.

My personal feelings ran deep, but I was also keen on marriage as a way of life; mine was a marrying generation. In my observation, single people, when they were not young men and women seeking to get married, were older people who had, to their disadvantage, not managed to do so. There was a phrase in common use, 'left on the shelf', which cruelly categorised the unmarried as people whom life had passed by. I knew that the phrase was applied to the two great woman teachers of my youth by those who did not respect their achievements. It seemed to me, however, that it applied most suitably to a sad middle-aged man who lived in a cramped little room off the verandah of the boarding house where we lodged while at the freezing works. Life at the mercy of the two draconic sisters who ran the place did not appeal as a possible future.

My sexual life, as is customary, began with the tentative approaches I made to one or two girls at school. At the Hastings boarding house I was seriously attracted to an older woman student also on seasonal work; she gained more satisfaction from an insurance agent living there. My close friends at university were male and, though we shared a lively interest in sexual matters, closeness, certainly in my case, did not go beyond the simply companionable. There were, of course, women in our Wellington circle but, again if only in my own case, relationships were thwarted by each party thinking (and of course hoping) that the other was the more experienced. I had, as well, a long-term girlfriend to whom I need, even at this late stage, to offer an apology for abruptly departing when my passion for Dorothy took hold. The hesitancy which characterised all these rather feeble strivings I can now see as a condition close to self-imprisonment; I do not think that I wanted, or could handle, a full and uninhibited relationship with anybody. I was still the same hesitant and incapable person when I married.

That Dorothy and I had met in a religious setting was appropriate and symbolic; throughout our lives, religion was both a shared concern and a source of unresolved differences. At the time we met I was, unlike her, still tiptoeing nervously around the edge of a religious commitment. She was a Methodist and, rather reluctantly, followed me first into Anglicanism in Oxford and into Catholicism many years later in Christchurch. But she insisted upon her independence; in each case we were 'received' in separate ceremonies.

We planned to leave for Oxford a few weeks after our marriage. It may have been especially imprudent to do so with scanty savings and the slender support of a scholarship worth £250 a year. But there were no hesitations; I was as intent upon marriage as I was upon Oxford. I was a successful junior lecturer and I had reason to think that I had a career ahead of me. About the same time I had graduated into the literary world and thought of myself as a writer with a future. The world was looking good and I was full of confidence. If Dorothy did not share it, she did not say so. Of course it was right to go, and our best years lay ahead. But this departure also initiated a long period of insecurity and unsettlement, hopping from place to place and house to house with a growing number of children.

After a few weeks living in a room rented from Peter Munz's mother, Carlotta (whose romantic photographic portraits date from this time), we boarded an awful little ship (I can never remember whether it was the *Mataroa* or the *Tamaroa*) in Wellington. My fare of £80 was covered by a free passage provided by the shipping companies for postgraduate students; Dorothy's parents paid for hers. We had a two-berth cabin well below sea level with a porthole glowing greenly at the end of a narrow passage. Pat Wilson, by a happy accident, was on the same ship in a cheaper many-berthed cabin at even lower depths. The three of us played canasta, a newish card game now forgotten, for much of the voyage, especially in the evenings with such drinks from the bar as we could afford. It was quite impossible to find cold drinking water; we believed this to be a plot on the part of the shipping line to force us to drink at the bar. It was said that the company paid the entire wage bill from the bar profits.

About halfway across the Pacific, beside a noticeboard on which the distance from New Zealand in the previous twenty-four hours was recorded, I found Dorothy in tears; it had just been borne in upon her how far she was from everything familiar. For the first time but by no means for the last, I found myself unable to deal with her grief. I had too easily assumed that the way of handling pain was to get away from its source; gradually I found this to be untrue. Dorothy's tears arose, I think, from a disturbance greater than any simple departure – from a deep and in the end inaccessible well of personal grief. She found some peace during our three years in England; we were never again as closely together.

Of course, the voyage was not all tears; we suffered from boredom much more than from grief, as the little boat limped its way across the ocean. Panama, in our innocence, we found exciting – the first foreign city we had seen. The three of us, Pat, Dorothy and I, walked around the strange streets, watched dark young women with a scrap of lace on their heads going in and out of the cathedral, drank beer in bars and ate food which seemed excellent after the drab regimen of the ship, and saw for the first time policemen in military uniforms carrying guns that they seemed all too ready to use.

It had taken three weeks to cross the Pacific, on a vessel so small that when she was tied up the upper deck was well below the level of the wharf.

We meandered through the canal, its forested banks littered with spent machinery. Then two weeks later we had sight of the southern shores of England, with its pastel-coloured, irregularly shaped fields climbing up and over the low hills beyond the cliffs, a civilised kind of nature that I recognised through a civilised kind of nature poetry, as well as through the memories I had absorbed from my parents. Wrongly, as it turned out, I supposed this to be the southern coast of Cornwall. But the mistake did not diminish the powerful double-take of mingled recognition and strangeness which began then and was to persist through all my experiences of England. That mix of the familiar and the foreign is, I came to believe, a profitable nexus in which to live, from which to think and feel.

The slow train journey from Southampton to Oxford provided a leisurely introduction to the patchwork of fields and copses, villages and towns. At length the train stopped for a brief period outside Oxford – a pause reputedly in memory of those nineteenth century dons who had for so long resisted the invasion of the city by the rail. There, across the gently up-and-down countryside, were the dreaming spires, a little blurred by the soon-to-be-familiar haze softening every prospect. We had arrived, but at what destination was always unclear. Oxford remained obscure to me both in its essence and its purpose. The place kept its glamour despite my quickly acquired familiarity with its harsh materialism; I lived there contentedly enough as one who had been given that entitlement, and yet as a perpetual stranger. Perhaps Oxford's gift to me was a prolonged experience of the benefits of what I had not yet learned to call hybridity – an inability and a disinclination to slough off either of my inheritances (from the old world and the new) even while experiencing in both a persisting element of strangeness.

Balliol College, the distinguished location to which Fred Wood's recommendation had gained me access, I found to be ambiguous and paradoxical: an ancient foundation housed in an unappealing neo-Gothic heap; a place of scholarship and learning given over to teaching a crowd of brattish ex-schoolboys; an institution which busily recruited postgraduate students and did not know what to do with them – and in fact did hardly anything. In time, I happily migrated to a place modern in foundation, in location (close to the railway station) and in buildings which, while unprepossessing, at least lacked ostentation – Nuffield College. My unrewarding attachment to Balliol was, perforce, retained, as Nuffield was not yet a college in the full legal sense. The residual ill-temper evident in this discourse arises, of course, from having been a fish out of water at Balliol; Nuffield was a postgraduate institution made up of students and fellows who came from all over the world – and if the water was not so many centuries deep, it was sufficient for my kind of swimming.

When, upon arrival, I presented myself at Balliol, I began inauspiciously, feeling thoroughly intimidated by an elderly man in a little room next to the entrance. I was to learn that he was the Head Porter, that he worked in the Lodge, and that he was a legendary person called Cyril. (He would, three years on, remove my little black gown, help me into my doctor's hired scarlet and blue, and relieve me of £1, a large sum at that time and in my straitened circumstances.) My first need was to secure a research topic and a supervisor. I was sent around from staircase to staircase and from door to door, and somewhere along the track left behind the idea of working in seventeenth century English history. I was given to understand (erroneously) that this field had already been too thoroughly ploughed over.

With happy memories of Halévy and even happier ones of Fred Wood, I turned to early nineteenth century England and may have paid a little homage to my father's politics by settling upon a trade union topic. That context was, after all, the working class England from which New Zealand had emerged, once the thin Wakefieldian crust of minor gentry had been broken, but I did not reflect upon that at the time. Balliol, it became apparent, could provide me with only a 'moral tutor', Hugh Stretton, a young Australian fellow, who assured me that my morals were of no concern to him. For supervision I found myself placed in the unenthusiastic hands of that 'unsociable socialist' G. D. H. Cole – a man I respected for his role in the history of British socialism as much as for his voluminous writings. I settled on a topic – the brief efflorescence in the heady early 1830s of ideas of a 'general union of the working classes' as the instrument through which an instant millennium, of sorts, would be achieved.

I saw Cole from time to time at All Souls, the most beautiful of Oxford colleges, and once, shaking with even more than my usual quota of social uncertainty, in his elegant house at Hendon outside London. He was not, as I found him, an easy or an agreeable man, but he was in a negative way a good supervisor: he left me more or less on my own. Once in a while I sent him draft chapters and he returned them with useful comments. One such draft, he told me, was distinctly good; I glowed when I read that. But the glow did not last. Not long after and well before I could finish, he republished (from an article in an obscure social history journal) a substantial but demonstrably, as I thought, inadequate monograph on the very subject of my thesis.

I thus learned an academic lesson which neither Wood nor Beaglehole had taught: that territoriality is part of the academic life. Cole was, of course, a prolific author; I relished a typically spiteful Oxford story of one don saying to another 'I see Cole has published his book again.' Petty of me, of course; but I found it quite impossible to publish a revised version of my thesis. Later I ground it into an article, quite possibly all the space these ideas required, for the *Economic History Review.* I hoped it might be published in time to back up my application for a chair; it duly appeared well into my first year in that position. Luckily, I concluded, jobs no longer depended on support from the Brits.

Apart from Nuffield and one or two other places of that kind, Oxford did not know what to do with the graduate students it attracted in some numbers. Balliol had no middle common room, and its junior common room seemed to be full of sweaty youths coming in from football to have their teas. I ventured into it a few times; on the first occasion I positioned myself beside a hatch from which I expected food and drink to emerge. It did not, and while I was looking around in some bewilderment a very English young voice from behind me inquired 'Are you in fact queuing?' I was, and moved on to where I should have been. I did not dare to have a meal in hall; in any case the food was said to be dreadful.

The college had a history society, named for Dervorguilla, the wife of one of the two founders, John de Balliol; at one meeting I was surprised to hear the youthful speaker refer to a medieval Edward (I cannot recall which) as 'one of our best kings'. The word 'our' gave me pause; in my customary environment it would not have been used. I attended the formal dinner of the society at which the guest speaker was one of my heroes, R. H. Tawney. The food was good, the company non-existent, as well as the wine, in deference to Tawney's abstemious habits. But Tawney was splendid; he explained his career in economic history by telling how, upon graduation, he became a tutor in adult education in Manchester and found himself puzzled by the modern world from which he had been sheltered, 'in particular by its economic arrangements'. That was worth the whole rather embarrassing evening.

Much of this account is testimony to my own deficiencies – though I do not count finding the English disagreeable among them. I was descended from an England that Oxford hardly knew, the England from which working people had emigrated in great numbers. Of course, plenty of New Zealanders and Australians – as well as bright working class boys from Britain itself – have made their peace with the ways of the English. They either absorb the establishment ethos or charge bluntly through it – or do both by turns, like Dan Davin, offspring of humble Irish emigrants and at that time the benign patron of a rather sketchily existing Kiwi Club. But that was not a way I wanted to follow, or could have followed. The example of those of my compatriots who have deracinated themselves by opting out of a whole segment of the given in their lives has confirmed me in the view that a kind of ambidexterity is best. Half a century on, the opposite kind of deracination has become a more urgent danger – that of opting out of the European inheritance into a dubious quasi-indigenousness.

Nothing in my upbringing, least of all the 'home country' habits I had acquired in my upbringing, had prepared me for the carefully nuanced distancing techniques with which the English regulated their social relationships. I did not at first realise that the phrase 'Oh, do you really think so?' was an invitation to conclude, not continue, a discussion. During a later spell in Oxford, Dan Davin explained to me that there were so many people in England that the English made an initial assumption that any new person would be boring; he added that in this they were for the most part right.

But the place was not an entire desert, though pleasurable academic occasions were infrequent. I went to a few lectures – an excellent series on utopian socialists attended by at least a dozen, at the first of which the lecturer hopefully enquired if this was where his audience really meant to be. And one delivered by the professor of poetry, Cecil Day Lewis, to a hall packed with young women, many from high schools: his romantically ravaged face, I thought, matched the expectations of his audience. My most vivid memory is of a joint seminar on the history of socialism conducted by G. D. H. Cole and Isaiah Berlin. Cole's tremendous solidity, wealth of information and total self-assurance offset, even if they did not quite match, the intellectual pyrotechnics of the unquenchable Berlin. At one point Berlin turned to Cole and said 'You surely do not believe that?' and Cole replied 'It is what I live by.' I forget the point at issue, but not the intensely human quality of the exchange and the sudden enlivening of the occasion to a point well beyond mere debate.

Research work brought many good moments to relieve its isolation and unavoidable tedium – documents discovered in unlikely places (one did not expect trade union pamphlets in the Bodleian, but there they were), sudden surprises at the end of a long and until then unprofitable day, turning over a file in the Public Record Office and finding pure gold that had no right to be under that label (reports from a government spy who had infiltrated my own special trade union), feeling that I had come to know and to like an eloquent and self-taught young journalist who wrote his editorials in (more or less) blank verse and died soon after the collapse of the union he had set all his hopes upon. Even more than the research itself, I enjoyed the ambience of those great repositories, the British Museum, the Bodleian Library and the Public Record Office, haunted by the dusty ghosts of the obscure scholars who had sat at those desks for what at the time seemed good reason and had passed on to a more lasting obscurity.

Outside the seminar room and the library, we found ourselves in the company of people like us, married postgraduate students whose college affiliations were not strong, usually from New Zealand and Australia, with (as time went on) small families starting up. Dorothy and I did a good deal together, and did it happily – exploring the neighbouring villages by bus and on foot, spending time in London with Pat Wilson and with Laurie and Dorothy Brown, discovering opera at Sadler's Wells and Covent Garden and taking in an occasional concert at the Festival Hall. Much of the time in London, while I was deep in the British Museum and the Public Record Office, Dorothy went to galleries and looked at old buildings. Often we ate and drank, very frugally, in pubs; my passion for pork pie dates from this time. Dorothy auditioned for the Oxford Bach Choir and was accepted; she was terrified by the ability of the young English people to sight-read instantly, but revelled in the B Minor Mass. She started rehearsals for Walton's *Belshazzar's Feast* but withdrew when pregnancy took her breath away. It was a good time; I am endlessly glad that we had it together.

We joined the small body of regular churchgoers (as distinct from the crowds flocking to special services) at St Mary's, the university church, and were confirmed in the Church of England. St Mary's was not High Church, but plenty of churches were; I (most often not 'we') went to Pusey House, the Cowley Fathers, Christ Church Cathedral and St Giles, defiantly ritualistic alongside the Martyrs' Memorial, all exemplars of the Anglo-Catholic movement, by that time (though I did not know it) past its peak. But it was good fun, 'holy fun' as I heard a parish priest call it. Laurie Brown, visiting from London and with a taste for liturgical variety, attended no fewer than eight ceremonies on a single Sunday, all quite different. Let Protestants go in for sermon-tasting; liturgy-tasting has its special pleasures and rewards. I have often thought, since, that the world would be a good and tolerant place if everyone was an Anglican of at least a moderate High Church tendency.

Cornwall, my other old world and one closer to my heart (if not my mind), was a more intimate but quite as ambiguous a matter. At first it seemed familiar but became increasingly strange as memory was supplemented by direct experience. We went to see my relations, mostly from my mother's family, in Truro and near Land's End. We stayed with my mother's sister, Auntie Janie, her husband Will and their clergyman son John Nicholls in Truro; my mother's cousins, John and Nan Williams and their children, at Roskestal in St Buryan; and (a short walk away but a fair distance socially) the cottage of my mother's childhood friend, Bertha

Jackson and her husband Charlie, in the little cove called Porthgwarra. I visited my father's sister, Aunt Maggie, living at Fraddon in a small, dark cottage with a large enamel teapot permanently on the hob. Here, a polite guest, I ventured upon a pipeful of her husband Howard's plug tobacco, an experience he probably knew would be alarming. The distance between the two family sets, in living conditions, social location, speech and habits, was considerable.

Time spent with these very dissimilar people turned my generalised 'Cornwall' into a set of divergent particulars. Ancestral images were translated from the early to the mid twentieth century; names and reputations became flesh-and-blood figures who could be agreed with or differed from, liked or disliked. The Cornwall of my childhood was assuredly there in concrete detail – the heather and furze running down to the granite cliffs, the abrupt fall of the cliffs to blue and white breaking waves, the golden sands of the little coves where we walked and gazed, the farmhouses where we sat down to enormous teas, the rows of bleak houses seen from the train on its way to those more romantic places – but it was forever changed by the shift from memory to experience. Every person and every place, every turn in the road, the cliff walks, the fields and hedges were immediately recognisable, but they became stranger than they had been when they dwelt only in an imagination formed by the memories of other people.

Through these encounters, the remembered and the experienced merged into a more complex whole. I retained, more emphatically than ever, a regard both for my mother's sturdy ideal of respectability and my father's determination to make things better. But now I was able to place these affirmations in a concrete social context of ranks and distinctions. I had sat down and eaten food in the humble cottage my father's sister occupied, not unlike those in which he had grown up. Closer to the middle of the scale was the neat suburban bungalow of my other aunt, my mother's sister, crammed with middle-class paraphernalia. A little higher were the farmers of the west country, some distinctly well off and others at least secure in tenancies which had descended from father to son. I had two glimpses of a yet higher social location, the manor house close to my father's village, and St Michael's Mount, now a castle and earlier a monastery. My cousin, taking us there on a visit, addressed the current occupant as 'My Lord', to my surprise. In these ways diffuse memories became a sharper recognition of privilege and its absence.

The ambivalence of my relationship to this society of distinctions and classes was made all the more real by the fact that I was living close to, though hardly within, that quintessential bastion of ancient privilege, Oxford University, much to my advantage – or so I hoped would be the case. It was this complexity that I tried to explore in the poem 'In the Fields of My Father's Youth' (which, to my surprise rather than my pleasure, became an anthology piece). The poem was something of a Procrustean bed into which I rather arbitrarily forced my experiences of emigration and re-migration. Even so, it helps me to recall what I thought about such matters in the early 1950s, or, perhaps, what I considered it appropriate to think about them. It hardly needs to be said that I do not think like that now. I have no problem about taking on board everything my father and my mother gave me and enjoying all the elements in the inheritance, including the conflicts and contradictions between them; they are integral parts of a fine and complex array of gifts.

While all this was going on in my mind, two material concerns demanded more attention: finishing my thesis and finding a job. The former was in my control, and a large tome was typed at great cost, bound in blue cloth and duly submitted for examination. I had a streaming cold on the day of the viva and arrived home to announce that I had forgotten the shopping but got the degree. I applied for many positions I am glad I did not get – one in Uganda, for which I was interviewed, unenthusiastically, the day after King Freddie of the Baganda was dethroned and a lasting chaos erupted. I wanted to stay in the United Kingdom and become a 'real' academic; when I failed in an application to Aberystwyth, a university college not far from the bottom of the heap, I concluded that New Zealand was probably my only, as well as a better, prospect. Two jobs quite suddenly surfaced, a senior lectureship at Victoria and a lectureship at Canterbury. Unwisely, as it turned out, I accepted the first offer that came; it was from Canterbury.

CHAPTER SEVEN

Finding a Country

We arrived in Christchurch in early 1955, after an arduous second-class voyage on a P&O liner to Sydney and a violent trip across the Tasman on that old rust-bucket the *Wanganella*, all the time keeping watch on an energetic small child. Our second son, Steven Mark, was only three months away. When, in the early morning after a night crossing on the ferry, we took a taxi from the railway station to her parents' home, Dorothy's tears as we passed through the too familiar streets were more bitter than they had been on the ship three years earlier. Within a few days I was on the phone to Wellington asking Fred Wood if the job from which I had withdrawn upon accepting the Canterbury position was still open. It was, but for one reason or other – among them my usual disinclination to cause an upset – I stayed at Canterbury. We settled for a year in a rented house next door to Sir James Hight, the venerable foundation professor of history and former rector of the university.

We were to remain in Christchurch for the next five years, in a succession of rented houses until we bought one. Built with inadequate foundations on the site of an old tip at the foot of the Cashmere Hills, it had already begun to sink and crack. The fact that the house had been inspected by Dorothy's clerk-of-works father and pronounced sound did nothing for family relationships. The family tie entailed dreary Sunday afternoon visits to the parental home – two longish bus trips there, two back, and the kids bored frantic in an immaculate suburban garden. Things were, of course, not like this all the time; there were good times, on the beach at Sumner, on the Port Hills, walking in Hagley Park, finding old friends and making new ones, and watching two children grow up.

The university was still reeling under the impact of the killing by the rector's young daughter and her close friend of the friend's mother. The rector, Henry Hulme, had resigned before this tragic event – one which has passed into New Zealand folklore through the film *Heavenly Creatures* – and no successor had yet been appointed. His term had been marked by dissent and acrimony; it was abundantly clear that the college continued to suffer from that experience. The department of history was also under strain; that energetic but uncomfortable man, Neville Phillips, had recently been appointed to the chair. He was intent upon licking into shape a department that he felt lacked rigour and discipline. This did not go down at all well with some of its members; for all that, and for all the troubles he experienced and at times invited during his tenure of the chair and his later vice-chancellorship, Neville Phillips, in the matter of academic direction, energy and exactitude, was an exemplary head of department.

In the first year I taught two papers and parts of two more; most were new to me. My segment of a history of political theory course was from Luther to Montesquieu (not, curiously, from Machiavelli to Rousseau). I dug out my old copy of Sabine, mugged up the main themes and, helped by not knowing too much, found again that I could give a good lecture. I have always been glad that this strenuous year forced me to discover American history in order to teach it, a useful prelude to New Zealand history. English history 'from Pitt to Peel' also fell to me – not unrelated to my Oxford research and to Halévy's great books. Each Monday I set out the week's lecture and tutorial notes in sequence in a folder and worked steadily through them, hardly raising my head during the week and greeting its end with relief.

In the second year, equipped with the previous year's lecture notes, I turned my mind to research and publication. I boiled my thesis down to book length but, as already sourly noted, it did not find a publisher. I was luckier with a couple of articles derived from the thesis; one found a home in *Oxford Economic Papers,* and the other in the popular *History Today.* This was on Robert Owen, and it prompted an English publisher to express an interest in a full biography. I cannot imagine what induced me to neglect this opportunity. More work in England would be required, but a start could have been made in New Zealand before leave came around. It was an odd decision, the first of a small series through which I passed up a chance to make a mark in a major scholarly field while trying to keep a little alive in it. A happier, if overly vain, reconstruction would be that some hidden hand was guiding me towards New Zealand history.

That call did come, in the form of an invitation from Fabers to write the New Zealand volume in their series on the countries of Great Britain and the Commonwealth. This was a surprise; I had studiously avoided New Zealand history and had opted for a field which I believed, snobbishly, to be in the mainstream of historical scholarship. My ignorance of this country's history was indeed great – I recall hearing Jim Gardner and David Fieldhouse, members of the history department, discussing a singularly devious and disreputable nineteenth century character and realising with a slight shock that they were talking about the man I still thought of as 'Good Governor Grey'.

Rashly, I accepted the Faber commission, started to do my homework (there was not all that much, in those days, to be done), submitted a sample chapter and became, at least prospectively, a New Zealand historian. By coincidence Keith Sinclair was writing his *History of New Zealand* for Penguin at this very time. I had known Keith a little in the 1940s, but then it was poetry, not history, that brought us together. His book was published in 1959 and my *Story of New Zealand* in 1960. He was also working on William Pember Reeves in the later 1950s; we swapped houses for a month, he to read Reeves material in the Canterbury Museum and I to read MA theses in the university library at Auckland. My sporadic but lengthy friendship with Keith, with its many ups and downs, lasted from that time until his death. In Auckland I certainly read a great deal, but I recall more vividly catching fish from a dinghy on Manukau harbour with Maurice Duggan, an experience which led to a poem about (roughly speaking) the King movement, published in the *Listener*, my first approach to Maori history and a small sign that New Zealand history had quite quickly taken root.

The two books are altogether unlike, quite apart from the fact that one author was an expert and the other an amateur. Sinclair's is nervy, energetic and staccato, and mine smooth, restrained and laid-back; his tone is nationalistic, and mine determinedly provincial. One could venture the guess that in some way the spirit of the times was at work. If so, it was a dual spirit; perhaps in these books two not readily compatible New Zealands each found an expression. Many years later, Keith Pickens argued that Sinclair had taken a Turnerian 'frontier' approach to New Zealand history and I a Hartzian 'fragment' approach. I had in fact not heard of Louis Hartz at that time, and Keith was quick to declare that he was not in the least influenced by Frederick Turner.

Nevertheless, Pickens's scheme is useful. The frontier theory emphasises the radical newness of societies on the edge of settlement, the dismantling of the inherited under the demands of an unpropitious environment, and the rebuilding of society from the ground up. There is a good deal of that in the Penguin *History*. The fragment theory emphasises the derivativeness of new societies, the way in which they transplant the characteristics of their parent societies at the time of establishment. Hartz goes on to argue that the transplanted characteristics are frozen in time at the point of foundation and can never significantly change, an untenable position which is not taken in the *Story*. In that book, however, the 'new' environment is represented as less than determinative and the inherited tradition as a formative and lasting influence on the emerging society.

On this slender basis one could construct a double vision of New Zealand in the 1950s as, on the one hand, radical, innovatory and awakening to its Pacific environment (Keith used to expand upon the similarities of California and New Zealand, mostly a matter of beaches and macrocarpas), and, on the other, as conservative, traditional and shaped by its foundational inheritance. Aptly enough, these two New Zealands were fashioned in Auckland and in Christchurch; further, the former was celebrated by a descendant of an early missionary and the latter by the child of recent immigrants. Each of us set out to explore a country which he needed to understand and explain, for his own sake and for that of his contemporaries, even if they were perceptibly different countries which, oddly enough, shared a single history.

The environment in which I wrote this history was distinctly colonial – a cluster of stone buildings, with courtyards and staircases that had been designed to recall the old English universities. My room was pokey, high up in a dank and inconvenient building with inadequate drains – but I looked from a dormer window over the trees lining Rolleston Avenue to the wide lawns and tall trees of Hagley Park. It was the most agreeable and the most work-conducive study I have ever occupied. (When the university shifted to suburban Ilam, two or three history lecturers considered staying behind, hoping that no one would ever notice.)

I was not really persuaded by the buildings and the parks that I was in an 'English' place; Oxford, despite the unlovely neo-gothicism of Balliol and the anonymous modernism of Nuffield, was too recent a memory. We lived in suburbs of bungalows and gardens which could hardly be mistaken for England in spite of their carefully chosen names – Fendalton, St Martins, Hoon Hay. Nevertheless, the city and its history, the university and its environs, the churches and public buildings, the naming of streets and squares, not only here but also in my faraway Feilding and Dannevirke, could and did prompt reflection upon the continuities in colonial development. Madras and Colombo Streets were not so named because they recalled places in Asia but because they were the names of Anglican dioceses. The effort of the colonisers and their successors to maintain continuity from homeland to colony and from the old to the new was evident enough.

The Story of New Zealand opened with a chapter on 'History and Habitat' and ended with one called 'Like and Unlike'. Although most of the space between was devoted to the delivery of information, this framework was intended to suggest a history shaped by the interaction of the deposit of inheritance and the modifying forces of environment. This model may well be dismissed as a passing 1950s fashion – one reflecting the vestiges of colonial dependence. However, fifty years later, it still seems to me a useful corrective to the contradictory and facile nationalism since popularised by PR people, politicians and arts administrators – contradictory because it simultaneously asserts that we have a national character and must busy ourselves finding out what it might be, and facile because it assumes that our inheritance can (and should) be sloughed off like a worn-out skin.

The material evidence of continuity between the old and the new, the centre and the periphery, was all around me, but intellectual influences had a greater effect in turning me more towards continuity than change. Neville Phillips's enthusiasm for Burke was infectious; the notion of society as an integrated, organic whole, held together by mutual dependence and respect for inherited values, was seductively appealing. Around this time Phillips reviewed, in the one essay, Keith Sinclair's *Origins of the Maori Wars* and Peter Munz's *Origin of the Carolingian Empire*, treating them as equally relevant to the history of New Zealand. This was to stretch the point a little, but only a little; today, the story often elicits looks of blank incomprehension or faint amusement.

Burke's influence met a serious check in the matter of politics. However much I was drawn to authority in general and a respect for social order, it was difficult to the point of absurdity to apply these notions to Sid Holland's New Zealand. But authority in matters of religion seemed, at least at this time, both more feasible and more attractive. I found the apparent solidity of the ex-colonial Anglican 'establishment' attractive; it seemed to provide additional evidence for the persistence of an ancient tradition. The elaborate ritual observances of Anglo-Catholic St Michael's, the 'mother church' of the Canterbury settlement and province, helped me to think of continuity and the persistence of the traditional as dimensions of the colonial experience.

My friendship with Charles Brasch also nudged me in the direction of tradition. Charles was not in the least troubled by matters of religion; without any fuss about creeds and observances he identified himself as a Jew and left it at that. But, as editor of *Landfall*, he regularly, indeed quarterly, insisted on the need to protect New Zealand's cultural inheritance, to defend it against Philistines in high political places, and to proclaim the role of culture as the guardian, indeed the purifier, of social values. He did not, as some would put it now, opt for the European alternative – such language would have been unintelligible to him, as in fact it is. He simply located New Zealand culture within a great and diverse European tradition. While he cannot be counted as a conservative in any political sense, he did fear for the well-being and even for the survival of tradition, especially in a society in which it had been attenuated by colonisation.

My need to explore tradition arose in part from a sense of personal insecurity that sent me on a search for safe harbours. I have no trouble with the view that a conservative approach begins from insecurity and from a realisation that social order is in itself a precarious achievement. Burke, after all, regretted having to defend traditional institutions with argument, for as soon as conservatism shifts from habit to justification it has lost the fight. I do not know that I saw things exactly like this in the 1950s, but the things I wrote then can reasonably be explained in this way.

This mood is more clearly manifested – not, I like to think, without a redeeming element of irony – in some poems I wrote around this time, especially one taking its departure from a distinctly 'real' Christchurch – the wind swirling autumn leaves down Rolleston Avenue and the smoke rising from fires in suburban gardens.

Autumn Fires

A slim girl on a bicycle
turns into a wind streaming with leaves,
divides with pertinent breasts
that tide of dissolution:
is a small image of heroism
refusing to die in the year's funeral
or merely to mourn, briefly, as the cortege passes;
yet even she may be hymned –

and the dull professor clad in a new car,
wrapped in a salary increase
heads off home through the leaves:

his prominent public brow rebuffs the season's menace;
and even he may be hymned, for a moment –

so too the children scuttering over the grass,
ignore the leaves, the beautiful gloom of the trees,
the season that nips their red cheeks
and the wind that carries their voices over the park –
though green fruit, are ripe for celebration.

Find room for them all on the bier, burn
with the slow salvoes of leaves
the long slim legs of the girl pounding her pedals,
the rump of the don printing the leather cushions,
the glittering limbs of the child.

Celestial gardener, heap
their accomplishments up for the burning:
for now there may not in the glance of your greater fire
survive either beauty or wit or strength;
all in their hurry are off
to a fire which you kindle everywhere and eternally.

This day, tonight, or at any time you choose
the trousered and sweatered girl will say Yes to your summons
and burn in the bed you've prepared,
and the aging don will see in the eyes of his children
the answer You will die soon, to the question he did not ask,
and the children will follow their fooling over the hedge
into a country blazing before their eyes.
It is always so, and for their well-being.

At the time Neville Phillips suspected that the 'dull professor' pointed to him. I demurred but did not entirely disabuse him; in fact I had John Garrett, the professor of English, in mind, more because he had a new car than because he was dull (which he was not).

In the same mood I finally put together a collection of poems, *Fire Without Phoenix*. I eliminated most of the more romantic and exuberant poems I had written previously, leaving those which were reticent and decorous. I celebrated the demise of the others in a concluding poem, using an extended image of refugees only a few of whom managed to escape into friendly territory:

> Those that were still left, dexterous escapers
> Theology caught with a withering burst of fire.
> And you, at the last, have straggled across the border.

The elegiac mood surfaces from time to time in the *Story*, but the book had a more concrete function. It was a commissioned project, and I was a professional; the publishers would be displeased if the story was told in a way which would deter readers. And, a necessitous young academic and family man, I was looking forward to the royalties. I did, however, indulge one stylistic idiosyncrasy. I had come to enjoy writing prose; this book, I determined, should be a piece of seamless prose, sentence upon sentence, paragraph upon paragraph, chapter upon chapter uninterrupted by quotations, section breaks, subheadings or footnotes. In this I was helped by the simple fact that there was not too much to know in the 1950s and thus little need to interrupt the flow with hesitations and reservations. Writing the book was a little like flying over the landscape in a light plane, cruising close to the ground where the evidence allowed and, when ignorance loomed like a threatening crag, climbing into the sky of handy generalisations. It was at least a manageable way of writing a general history.

The decade which began with my return to New Zealand in 1955, living first in Christchurch and then in Wellington, had an inward-looking character, at least for me. Once the turbulence of the 1951 waterfront dispute was out of the way and the cold war, after the Korean crisis, had settled into a kind of uneasy normality, there was little to divert my attention from my inner and my immediate concerns, especially in the early 1960s, as more children were born. From around this time Peter Munz recalls a conversation in which I grumbled that as my children grew more I grew less. Even so, an inability to leave things alone took me into public concerns – oddly enough, in the light of my drift towards conservative opinions, on the radical side. Some habits are too deeply ingrained to be altered by mere ideas; in Christchurch I voted for Mabel Howard and in Wellington for a Labour lawyer with a shady past who stood against the impeccable John Marshall.

In the later 1950s I was a member of the public affairs committee of the Christchurch Anglican diocese with, among others, Jack Vaughan, a professor of chemistry with a wide interest in social and humanistic concerns, and Norris Collins, secretary of the railwaymen's union, who embodied the tradition of tough-minded moderation which characterised the Christchurch labour movement. This committee joined the campaign against the death penalty, abolished in 1941 and restored in 1950 by the National government. During the 1950s Marshall, the Attorney-General, earned the nickname 'Hanging Jack' for his persistent refusal to commute the penalty. Labour, in opposition, almost succeeded in abolishing it on a free vote. Holland, anxious to retain the penalty, proposed to hold a referendum at the time of the 1957 general election. Abolitionists, convinced that a referendum would entrench the death penalty by enlisting massive public support, agitated against it for that very reason; the people should not be encouraged to speak when they are likely to get it wrong.

The diocesan committee waited upon Harry Lake, a local MP and a future Minister of Finance, and urged him to use his influence against the referendum. He was clearly sympathetic to the committee's argument. In the event, the government gave up the idea. Another free vote, in 1961, removed the death penalty (except, quaintly, for the crime of treason). My personal contribution to the debate was to invite George Hughes, professor of philosophy at Victoria University and an Anglican priest, to write on the matter for *Landfall*. He undertook to show that though the taking of human life could be justified in some situations, the punishing of a person found guilty of murder was not among them, because the desired end could be attained by less irreversible means.

At that time I was standing in for Charles Brasch as editor; after bringing *Landfall* out four times a year for ten years, he took a spell overseas. We had seen a good deal of each other after I returned; our children loved him and called him 'Chiles'. He left me with the task of bringing out one issue and preparing copy for the next – my first real experience of editorship.

Charles was an interventionist editor, especially with poems, and the country was full of poets, myself among them, who had been irritated by his suggestions for improvement. I tried this with some poems Jim Baxter sent in. The exchange ended quite amiably with him, in his own words, kicking and snarling and not giving way an inch. The hard work in editorship was with the essays, commentaries and reviews; they had to be chivvied out of busy people and often there was a need to turn sows' ears into silk purses. Charles did not approve of all aspects of my stewardship, notably the inclusion of some poems I solicited from my friends in Wellington, but he was far too gentle to say so until, later on, I commented unfavourably upon something in another issue. 'Well,' he burst out, 'I don't think you should have published those poems of Erik Schwimmer's!'

By this time I had been connected with small (and often ephemeral) publications for many years. *Hilltop* and *Arachne* were good fun and yet quite seriously meant; this publishing venture ended only on shipboard as I left Wellington in 1951. Hubert Witheford and Erik Schwimmer pursued me to make one last try to collect a substantial – for those days – sum of money I was reckoned to owe the enterprise, not by way of a debt but the unpaid value of shares in the Crocus Publishing Company, a limited liability company which had been formed to protect those who, like Hubert, were householders from being sold up. The final siren warning all visitors to leave saved me and my money. That was the last I had to do with the financing of any publication. In Christchurch in the mid 1950s, and in spite of my Anglo-Catholic opinions, I became editor of the Student Christian Movement journal, *Student*. The SCM secretary, Pat Morrison, supplied the in-house material and I collected notes and articles. I recall only a few items – for example, the set of responsive prayers I wrote for an SCM meeting and printed in the journal, in part an experiment with form based upon the Prayer Book. And for the first time I encountered the rich smell of hot metal, filling the old-time printing works down an inner city alley when I went to collect and return the galleys.

The late 1950s brought an end (inevitable perhaps) to my prolonged love affair with John Henry Newman. While I enjoyed the High Church observances at St Michael's, a niggling doubt as to the authenticity of the Anglo-Catholic position had taken root. Could a tolerated minority, widely regarded as eccentric within its own church, really embody the universalist claims of Catholicism? Not, it seemed to me in the end, at all convincingly. Later I could see Newman's long anguish, poised between Canterbury and Rome, and his horror at looking into the history of the early church and recognising himself as a heretic, as a moving and exciting story rather than as a pilgrim path to be followed. Even then I suspected that these concerns and anxieties were, historically, a late flurry of a nineteenth century crisis of belief – and, personally, a disinclination to take control of my own life.

So, at the end of the 1950s G. H. Duggan, the Catholic chaplain at Canterbury College and a well-known controversialist, received me into the Roman Catholic church, after a conditional baptism of a most unceremonial kind with the holy water conveyed in a cracked glass jug. Not long thereafter I found myself with a small child outside a firmly closed school; it was, it dawned upon me at length, St Patrick's Day. As Vincent O'Sullivan commented, I had a lot to learn. Some I learned after I had taken on the editorship of *Comment*. The journal emerged from discussions with Betty O'Dowd, a lecturer in history (and the first of a number of women who radically altered my thinking about those aspects of the world we shared and more especially about those we did not), Bernard Smyth, an extension lecturer at the university, and Pat Downey, a Wellington lawyer and future Human Rights Commissioner.

Comment announced itself as 'liberal Catholic' and offered to provide New Zealanders in general with a forum for the discussion of political and social concerns. It was never a 'confessional' journal – in fact, so much was this not the case that some of its supporters became uneasy, especially when later it fell into the hands of people whose Catholicism was less doctrinaire, such as Vincent O'Sullivan and Harry Orsman. About the same time and also in Christchurch some good old socialists, led by Winston Rhodes and Wolfgang Rosenberg, founded the *New Zealand Monthly Review,* also moderate and accommodating in spirit but clearly on the other side of the ideological divide. For there was a divide; these were not the years of the cold war for nothing. When I went to see the Catholic bishop to tell him what some of his flock were proposing, an attendant priest said, 'We must make use of our intellectuals, my lord', and some financial support followed. I doubt if it was an investment in the liberal cause. The first number of *Comment* appeared in 1959; it moved with me to Wellington a year later and I ceased to edit it only when I departed for Palmerston North in 1964. The first series went on until 1970; its revival in 1977, by a group of Massey staff, was prompted by alarm at the degeneration of political debate under Robert Muldoon; this second series lasted until 1982.

In 1959, as my time in Christchurch drew to a close, *The Story of New Zealand* was also nearing completion. I typed up the handwritten draft (a splendid way of revising) and sent chapters out for comment. Neville Phillips, who took a great pride in the publications being written by members of his department, was sharp and useful. Writing from Wellington, Fred Wood made many not readily decipherable marginal comments (one I still treasure: 'A touch of A+ here!'). The final typescript had to be professionally typed. I approached the registrar (the department did not have a secretary) only to be turned down: the university could not meet the cost of a book which would earn money. I entered into a private arrangement with one of the registry typists. She did a good job, paradoxically enough in her spare time during office hours.

The book did make a good deal of money; it got me a senior lectureship at Victoria in 1960 and helped me to get the Massey job a few years later. It also brought me my first royalties of any consequence. The Caxton Press had sent me a cheque for 12*s* 6*d* for *Fire Without Phoenix*; for many years I preserved both the cheque and the royalty statement in my papers. The advance royalties from Fabers were real money; they met that part of the price of a new car which had then to be found in sterling funds. I had driving lessons and got my licence. We took delivery of the bright little grey Mini – our first car and only new one ever. Symbolically perhaps and grievously for sure, I did in the grill within a few days, not braking quickly enough driving down Kelburn Parade by the university.

We moved to Wellington at the beginning of 1960 – the year that the *Story* was published. With our two children we found a rented house in Island Bay; the next two, William Hugh and Thomas David, were born with some promptitude within three years. I became ever more committed (over-committed) to teaching and publishing. Work was, for a time, a haven.

Now that I can look back, with the help of an alarmingly detailed bibliography compiled to greet me on my seventy-fifth birthday, my writing in these years strikes me as prodigal, even profligate. Poems regularly appeared in *Landfall* and the *Listener*; I squeezed a handful of professional articles out of my poor thesis; I wrote many reviews – there was nothing between two covers I would not have a go at – and notes and essays for *Comment*. I seem to have been unable to leave anything alone: I wrote on the ecumenical movement, New Zealand and the Pacific, university growth and university fees, state aid to private schools, religion in schools, the politics of South East Asia, trade unions, the Labour Party, the 1963 election, broadcasting policy and, I now find it hard to credit, the problems of youth. But I do remember with pleasure an obituary on 'Sir Sydney Holland' (rightly marked '[sic]' in the bibliography); I had planned to entitle it 'Death of a Salesman' but chickened out at the last moment. I have been surprised to find that I had the nerve to review Keith Sinclair's Penguin *History* and his *Origins of the Maori Wars*. However, by the time I reviewed his *William Pember Reeves* I had got the Liberal period sufficiently together to have a right to an opinion. That review led to a longer essay, 'Reeves, Sinclair and the Social Pattern', published in 1969 in *The Feel of Truth*, a festschrift for Fred Wood and John Beaglehole edited by Peter Munz. When Erik Olssen used it as a chopping block for an argument about the nature of class in New Zealand, it became the beginning of a rare historiographical debate.

I can still look back composedly upon a *Landfall* review of G. H. Scholefield's edition of *The Richmond–Atkinson Papers*. The published text struck me as curious in places; upon inspecting the originals I found that the editor had not only made mistakes in transcription (a venial sin) but had defaced the manuscripts with overwriting and instructions to his typist (a mortal sin, or at least if it isn't it should be). He had, of course, been editor of the first *Dictionary of New Zealand Biography*; when I became editor of its successor I found myself obliged to write his entry, because no one else would. These coincidences prompted Frances Porter – who should have written it – to remark that I was the only person known to have killed his predecessor, succeeded to his position and written his obituary.

At Victoria I taught half of the two-paper New Zealand history course and an honours paper, and supervised graduate theses, one of the chief delights of my later academic years. The New Zealand course was an exciting venture, and a risky one, for the research and publication base remained thin. Much depended upon lectures, and they in turn depended upon a renewed reading of MA theses. I had never enjoyed lecturing so much before, nor have I since. New Zealand history was still a matter of fresh discovery; I was, in sober fact, continuing with the project of finding a country by thinking about it – adding historical information and interpretation to personal experience and reflection. I paced the front of the lecture room, like (I was later told) a speaker on the marae. But marae, at that time, were outside my experience.

In this class I encountered my first Maori students, two young men from the extensive Hawke's Bay Bennett family. One talked to me about the responsibility he felt for his people, and deplored the frivolity of the other, who ran a dance band, Teddy Bennett and his Bears I think it was called. Half a century later I watched a TV programme on Maori in Australia – here was the musician Bennett, now a quite different kind of leader, talking about the recovery of language and culture among Sydney Maori. In those untroubled years, however, Maori figured little in the minds of most Pakeha, except defensively, when someone like the impudent American, David Ausubel, accused them of prejudice and discrimination.

Over the decade since returning to New Zealand I had, rather more by accident than design, gone through a process which might be called intellectual naturalisation. When, in 1954, the *Wanganella* rounded North Cape and crept down the eastern coast to Auckland, a few returners huddled together on the deck and watched the coast slip by with mingled feelings of recognition and gloom. The gloom has never quite gone away; the recognition has grown in breadth and depth from that time to the present. Within a decade or so, with due allowance for all that was yet to be learned, I had found my country.

CHAPTER EIGHT

An Expanding Horizon

Finding a country was, for me, essentially a matter of recognising more and more clearly the nature and character of the place where my life began, where it continues and where it is likely to end. That widening and deepening process of recognition continued throughout all the ways of living with history which I explored from the 1960s to the end of the century, from my late thirties to my late seventies; it has not yet ended. I did not, of course, solemnly pledge to undertake that task; a saving grace of scepticism has saved me from such highmindedness. Nevertheless, a succession of decisions – to apply for the Massey professorship, to bring out the *Oxford History*, to take on the *Dictionary of New Zealand Biography*, to get into (and out of) Waitangi Tribunal business and to write this book – taken together fall into a pattern. Things have happened as if that shadowy hidden hand which first beckoned me into New Zealand history was still urging me on.

This imperative, however it may be explained, committed me to an expanding range of activities in teaching, administration, research, writing, editing and publishing. These make up a rather disparate bundle of undertakings, which either relate or give way to the need to explore the past of the country which I could no longer imagine not belonging to. From the mid 1960s to the early 1980s these pursuits were followed in what seemed to many an unpromising location, a small university college just outside the minuscule metropolis of my infancy, Palmerston North. (I reminded those who pointed this out to me that in the early sixteenth century a good deal had been achieved by an obscure professor at Wittenberg, also a provincial university.) Peter Munz, one who had always travelled on, from Germany through half a dozen other countries to New Zealand, warned me of the danger of a shrinking vision if I returned to my place of origin. He was wrong; Massey provided me with an expanding horizon. For the first time I was running my own show; though I could not do just what I liked, what I could do was my own.

The decision to apply for the Massey job arose from more mundane considerations; quite simply, we needed money. We had left Christchurch almost penniless after selling our house at a loss. In Wellington we had to rent; when our fortunes began to improve, we thought about buying again. The best we could expect would be a house in a distant suburb, say, Johnsonville. It was not difficult to conclude that a small city with more money would be better than an outlying suburb with less. History chairs were due to be established at Massey and at Waikato; I decided to apply for the first one to come up. I have always been glad it was at Massey.

Before the position was advertised, I had delivered at Massey a memorial lecture celebrating the extraordinary life and career of Donald Anderson. With a glance at Simkin's economic history, I called it *The Inadequacy of a Dependent Utopia,* and explored in a rather Braschian fashion both the limitations and the benefits of being a part of a larger whole, of being a province. I did not mean a province of Great Britain – the fall of Singapore was a recent memory and the British effort to join the Common Market a current context – but a 'provincial' dependency upon the greater powers and cultures among which our lot was cast. It turned out to be a pre-inaugural lecture; by the time it was published I had been appointed foundation professor of history.

Fred Wood was on the appointment panel; as we were both going to the interview, even if to sit on opposite sides of the table, I took him in the little grey Mini and put him down at a decent distance from the interview room. He was quite taken with the irregularity of this procedure. In the interview the vice-chancellor, Alan Stewart, put a question about the purpose and use of history – with two professors of history in the room, he said, he might get a good answer. Fred was careful to stay silent; I had the impression that my reply was too long and too involved to be convincing. But that did not matter; Alan Stewart was a supremely practical man – a university had to have arts subjects (so everyone then, if they have not since, believed), and history was one of them.

Going to Massey at that time was a matter of contingency and chance, good luck and good timing. I was one of that numerous body of academics of the post-war generation who were able to climb the ladder more quickly than had been possible before or has been since. My good luck had held, and not just because I was able to make my run to the top in a sellers' market; I could not have ended up in a better place for what I was discovering I wanted to do. At first I did not see it that way; I had never been in a job for more than five years and I expected that pattern to continue. Though I tried twice to leave before the 1960s were out, I was to stay at Massey for nearly twenty years. Literally, I grew old in the job.

Massey was a down-to-earth place, intimately involved in the economic and social life of New Zealand – some would say, as I did at the outset, too much involved for its own good. Alan Stewart's question – 'What is the use of it?' – was one I was never able to ignore in my Massey years. Nor was I able to answer in any but an unconvincing way; in the end I realised that the value of the question lies in the absence of any final answer. There are many things we regularly do which we cannot account for in those terms; attempts at utilitarian answers only lead to the same question all over again. Massey, an institution dedicated to making two blades of grass grow where one grew before, was a splendid place in which to learn that history (and a host of things we cannot do without) has nothing at all to do with growing grass. The better question is 'Why do we do history, in spite of its lack of utility?' The only answer I have ever found is a bit circular – something like 'Because people want to.'

The notion that universities should earn their keep by being useful was not altogether foreign to me. I could see, when I worked there, that engineering at Canterbury and law and commerce at Victoria were ways in which those institutions had set out to serve their communities. But many in the arts, all through the New Zealand university system, felt a certain disdain for such considerations. I remember the lofty contempt with which some of us at Canterbury greeted George Jobberns's remark that his geography department existed as a service to school teachers. And, at Victoria, some of us rejoiced in the remark ascribed to Tommy Hunter, that it would be a sad day when the college was not at odds with the business community (the city worthies had been offended by some obscenity in a student Extravaganza). I am still inclined to question Jobberns and to applaud Hunter (if indeed he ever said it), but at Massey I learned that such an above-the-battle attitude was neither politically useful nor – of greater importance – socially responsible.

Inevitably, a university institution founded to bring science to agriculture, which took pride in its achievements in pasture management, dairy science and animal husbandry, which honoured William Riddett, Percy McMeekan and F. W. Dry, was one in which practical questions were always in the air. The two faculties with which I was associated, Humanities and Social Sciences, came into existence at the same time as the Veterinary School; not long before that Agriculture had given birth to Food Science and Biotechnology. The new Science Faculty gave pride of place to the biological sciences. On the fringes, the university paid attention to such items as wool, leather, poultry and pigs. Maybe it could be argued that the world was too much with us; but it could not be said that history and the arts did not feel a need to have their feet upon the ground. And though I was among those who, at first, did not care to admit it, that ground was the situation of students who were unable to attend a university.

Whatever we might have thought about the ultimate value of all those things we held closest to our hearts – the study of poetry, of Renaissance politics, of British colonial policy, of logical positivism, or of religious certainty – we had to accept the fact that our function was to look after extramural students. There would have been no arts teaching had not students who were exempted from lectures been handed over, first to Palmerston North University College, the short-lived branch of Victoria

University, and thence to Massey. The needs of school teachers for further qualifications, of housewives in suburbs and small towns for some exercise of the mind, and of people all over the country for a new start, provided a sufficient justification for our existence. Meeting their needs might not have been a complete answer to the question of utility, but that, really, was their affair. If they found our courses valuable, it was our job to teach them. This was the beginning, too, of my own awareness that the study of history, for one reason or another, was seriously pursued by a great number of people out there in the cities, the suburbs, the small centres and the countryside.

Odd as it must seem, now that a small army of tertiary providers has joined in the scramble for distance education, extramural study was then viewed with suspicion. When in the 1960s and 1970s I visited other universities, I met an attitude of amused contempt and tolerant compassion because of my involvement in such a low form of education. Things have indeed changed; the need to get out there and bring in business is now acknowledged by most universities and a host of other agencies; Massey was simply first. But I saw little of this at the time; I was among the many who argued that 'true' university teaching was face to face (even if several hundred learning faces confronted one teaching face) and that the diluting effect of postal tuition should never be allowed to spread across an entire degree. I adhered to these principles in history teaching until near the end of my time at Massey; in spite of the later opening of the floodgates – maybe just because of that – I still believe that there is something to be said for caution in these matters.

In my first year, I was given an opportunity to fly my conservative flag. The Catholic chaplain, Fr Godfrey, sought to make the Catholic presence felt by holding an academic 'red mass' in St Patrick's church, with elaborate ceremony and an archbishop. A sizeable number of university staff turned out in their regalia and, after the archbishop had dismayed his audience by preaching for the best part of an hour, repaired to the church hall for a fine supper. There, as if the audience had not been sufficiently exercised, I was to give an address. I enlarged upon the dangers of extramural study and urged Massey not to imperil university education and its own reputation by going overboard. The vice-chancellor was not pleased; I was summoned to his office and asked (politely and yet a little ominously) if I proposed to give the same speech to a Rotary Club I was addressing that week. I said that I was not – which was true. No more was said; I was left reflecting that at least you knew where you were with Alan Stewart, and that where I should be was not a position likely to jeopardise the development of history at Massey.

It was not easy to persist with the view that extramural teaching was bound to be second-rate. Vacation courses at Massey, I soon found, were among the most satisfying teaching experiences I had ever had. These students, no longer young and usually with family and community responsibilities, were not in a mood to waste time or money. I finished one long weekend packed with lectures and tutorials, sitting exhausted on a high stool after the closing session, shaking hands with the departing students; they thanked me and I felt I should be thanking them. One elderly woman enrolled to support her daughter who was seriously lacking in self-confidence. The daughter managed a pass, but her mother turned out to be a straight A student. When she finished her BA, I urged her to enrol in the honours course. No, she said, she would not do that; she wanted to catch up on the many books in her undergraduate courses that she had not had time to read. Not at all second-best and very far from second-rate.

We ran classes in other centres, usually in university premises. At the University of Waikato (which had decided not to cater for part-time students in its early years), we drew more local students than there were in the university's equivalent courses. Once in Auckland, looking down at Wynyard Street from the balcony of the history department building, I watched a stream of well-to-do-women turn up for my class in expensive cars. No, they told me, they would not prefer to be internal students; the library was useless and one lecture took three hours, what with driving and looking for a park, if you were lucky enough to find one. They were good students, mature and self-motivated, influential in their neighbourhoods and a PR asset to any university which gave them an honest dollar's worth. After a few years the other universities, with shaky enrolments and enfeebled finances, began to court them. Eventually, when I visited other universities, I found myself discussing their plans for distance education.

At Massey the numbers of internal and external students steadily increased and with them staff numbers; in these liberally financed years more students meant more staff. The history department became large enough to teach a reasonably wide curriculum. It was designed around the twin themes of environment and inheritance. Students could concentrate on either European (including English) history or New Zealand and the Pacific; because there was no 'canon' and no restriction on choice, they could (and many did) opt for a mix of the two streams. We were looking for an area of specialisation which would give the department a distinctive character, and found it in the history of the Pacific Islands. No New Zealand university was offering more than an isolated paper in that field – a curious gap, considering how closely the country had been related to these islands since the nineteenth century. We recruited staff from Jim Davidson's Pacific history school at the Australian National University and developed a sequence of papers which extended from the first year to postgraduate level.

By the early 1970s there were enough students to justify an honours degree. Research for the degree was, for the most part, steered towards relatively neglected aspects of New Zealand history, especially the period which had come to fascinate me, the Liberal era. There was some groundbreaking research in labour, agriculture, welfare and women's history (by students who are today senior academics, Peter Gibbons, Tom Brooking, Charlotte Macdonald and Margaret Tennant among them) and some useful studies in the history of Woodville, Pahiatua, Feilding, Palmerston North and Hawke's Bay. Students were encouraged to follow their own interests. One was a keen rugby player, who often turned up for Monday classes patched with sticking plaster; his eyes brightened at the suggestion that he might like to investigate the social structure of rugby in the Manawatu. Another, a huge and slightly forbidding man commonly dressed in singlet, torn-off jeans and jandals, found his research into social stratification in Feilding impeded by the refusal of the Rangitikei Club even to let him in the door, let alone use their records. How, I enquired, was he dressed when he showed up at the club? His next request was more successful.

When in 1969 the University of Otago invited me to deliver the Hocken Lecture (published two years later as *Towards a New History?*), I used the occasion to argue for an historical perspective which went beyond the 'four main centres' to take in the country's regions and localities. It would, I said, lead to a 'new' New Zealand history. I am glad that I added a query to the title, for the continuing growth of regional and local histories has not led to any such revision. New Zealand regions have not differed all that widely from each other and the distinctive characteristics of their initial European settlement have diminished over time. The inclusion of the regions in a general story is a matter of simple historical justice – in some respects like giving a rightful place to the histories of Maori, women, ethnic minorities and children. In some respects, but not all – for a fuller investigation of the past as experienced by both Maori and women alters the nature of the wider history. It was for such reasons that I put into place a broad programme for selection (and research) in the *Dictionary of New Zealand Biography*, to the alarm of some elitists.

A proposal from the rather grandly entitled East Coast Development Research Association soon gave me the chance to practise what I preached. I accepted their invitation to write a history of the region for the bicentenary of Cook's arrival in Poverty Bay in 1769. I was not so innocent that I neglected to insert in the agreement a provision which required me only to consider, and not necessarily to heed, any representations the association might make about the text of the book. This turned out to be a wise, though not quite an adequate, precaution; I learned that authors of sponsored books should never relax their vigilance.

The association was intent upon promoting the region in every possible way, political, economic and ideological. The history was to serve this purpose by establishing the East Coast as a place with a distinctive character and history. I had no problem with that part of my brief. The association had already sponsored a land use survey – a substantial publication which described the current character and use of land in order to provide a basis for improving efficiency in the future. This was part of a campaign to convert to exotic forestry all the back country inland from what became the notorious 'blue line' – notorious because a good deal of that land was in Maori ownership and the association was not much inclined to consultation. Another ill-founded plan was to set up a factory to produce cigarette filters from maize; the local MP, Esme Tombleson, was especially enamoured of this proposal. No one, as far as I can recall, thought of grapes, the one crop that flourished as all the others fell away.

This background helps to identify the context in which sponsored history may and usually does go on, even if in less obvious ways. The mayor of Feilding later on approached me to discuss a history of that town: we have, he said, nothing to give visitors except a teaspoon. Boosterism was endemic in colonial towns and remains one of the most persistent colonial survivals. In the course of my East Coast researches I came across a newspaper report in which the writer, surveying the handful of masts in Gisborne's perpetually troublesome harbour, reflected on a future in which it should have become the Liverpool of the Pacific. But there was also a good deal of redeeming humour – the story of a horse-drawn coach which disappeared into a pothole on the road south and did not emerge for several days – and some strong doses of backblocks realism. I found myself on the side of the realists and this, in the end, did not make me many friends in the region.

I set about writing a history of settlement and race relations, as we then called it, and one which excluded the centuries before colonisation. I have not yet quite abandoned the attitude I then effortlessly assumed, that prehistory is all very well in its way but real history begins with documents. This may be because my own prehistory is on the other side of the world; I had certainly scrambled around ancient remains in Cornwall with a strong feeling of belonging. There was, however, plenty of taha Maori in the book. Through the excellent research of my assistant, Jane Thomson, the story of Maori enterprise and initiative emerged as a central theme in the early part of the history, a pattern I was able to recognise more fully when Ann Parsonson wrote her chapter 'The Pursuit of Mana' for the *Oxford History of New Zealand*. And it was soon borne in upon me that if the East Coast had produced one great man in the settlement period, it was either Te Kooti Arikirangi or Rapata Wahawaha. Today I would not be sure which to choose, but then I was on the side of Te Kooti.

This enthusiasm served me well years later when I addressed the New Zealand Maori Council on the *Dictionary of New Zealand Biography*. How, one suspicious questioner asked me, would I deal with such a figure as Te Kooti? I was able to reply that I had already had a shot and was glad when another council member said 'And a good one too.' But the Pakeha mandarins of the East Coast were another matter. I had realised that they did not have much to do with Maori after my requests to meet Henry Ngata came to nothing. In the end I walked into his Gisborne office, introduced myself and was politely received. We had a useful discussion, as I did with the Ngati Porou historian, Rongo Halbert, on his sickbed but full of authority and presence.

None of this prepared me for a party at which I was plied with whisky (for which my tolerance had by that time become considerable) and told: 'We must set you right, Bill, on Maori land.' What my hosts meant was that Maori land had been left to go to rack and ruin and should be taken away for forestry. Ironically, the association's own land use survey enabled me to compare a map of land ownership with one of land utilisation. The conclusion was clear – both Maori and Pakeha land had deteriorated under unfavourable conditions of terrain and location. When I received proofs of the book from the *Gisborne Herald*, I found that a sentence saying that Maori land and deteriorated land did not coincide had been transformed by the deletion of the word 'not'. I put it back; it stayed there.

After three years at Massey I decided that I had to get away from the daily round of teaching, committees and agenda papers. In 1967 I took a few months' leave in Oxford, and left my family behind; Dorothy was pregnant and understandably resentful. (I did return in time for the birth of Elizabeth Mary, but with little to spare.) I had a research topic ready to go; in the 1950s I had been intrigued by Robert Owen's references to his mission as a kind of Second Coming and by the mood of millennialist expectancy in the trade unions and co-operatives. I proposed to look at the occurrence of such quasi-theological ways of thought in political and social movements that we would normally regard as secular. But Gisborne and New Zealand were still close to hand; I kept being reminded that Te Kooti and the Maori prophetic movements would have been recognisable, perhaps with some bemusement, by the English millennialists of the early nineteenth century.

Once I was set up at Nuffield, with all the time and research resources in the world close to hand, I found it alarmingly difficult to settle down to work. I struggled to keep my attention on pamphlets, sermons and theological tomes. I had become almost incapable of reading anything not poorly cyclostyled on low-grade paper. I listened to talk of the college fellows and envied them for the meetings they grumbled about and the politics in which they evidently delighted. That was the academic life which I was acutely missing. Often, then and since, I have reflected on the comment uttered by Alan Crowther, the sardonic professor of psychology I had known at Canterbury in the 1950s – 'Why do academics turn from scholarship to administration? Because it is easier.' He had.

But after a while I took off. I set out for the Bodleian first thing; came back to Nuffield for a lunch substantial enough to be my main meal; went back to the library and worked till early evening. I commonly ate a burger and walked around suburban streets as darkness fell, looking enviously into warmly lit uncurtained rooms. Often I went to evening mass and sometimes to confession. I sensed, even through the grill, the weary contempt with which the youthful priest greeted my peccadillos. I wonder, now, if one so uneasy in the presence of human inadequacy had much of a future in the church – not, I suspect, a good one for those in his care. Back at Nuffield, I went over my notes and photocopies, scribbled a few draft passages, went to the common room for late-night TV and perhaps a pint, and slept like a log. Until the next day, and the next ... I let nothing, not even an invitation to join a canal holiday in Ireland, disrupt this schedule. It was the nearest I have come to the life of a celibate, almost a monastic, scholar; I can report that it is indeed a good life for a time but, as Newman said of life in general, in the end it does not satisfy.

On the way back, I spent a couple of weeks in the United States, chiefly to visit John Pocock at Washington University in St Louis. There was a chance of a job there, teaching British history according to the Pocockian prescription – roughly, the British everywhere they had set themselves down, including New Zealand. The history department was the most agreeable and companionable academic community I had ever mixed with; no doubt the situation was one to bring out the best in us all. The idea was immensely attractive – as was that of living in one of those well-to-do leafy suburbs where most university people dwelt. But not too well-to-do, I was advised. The Vietnam war was warming up and the children of resident aliens were included in the draft; we had two sons in their early teens. Choose, said my prospective colleague, a very sweet man of whom I had at once become fond, a locality with a sufficient population of Afro-Americans and Puerto Ricans to fill its quota. That, I thought, is a kind of corruption I can do without. The idea that our sons might end up in Vietnam, together with a reluctance to see the children grow up American and, as well, my renewed discovery that I feared change more than standing still, led to a regretful letter declining the offer.

By the mid 1960s Vietnam had become a burning issue in New Zealand as the country drifted into a commitment to join the United States in supporting the South Vietnam regime. My participation was limited to a 'mobilisation' demonstration on the streets of Palmerston North (in a manner typical of the inhabitants of a provincial city we told each other that, *per capita*, it was the largest in the country) and to speaking at 'teach-ins' at Auckland and Victoria universities, with Keith Sinclair and Robert Chapman. These were exhilarating occasions; the government sent Leslie Monro to one and Keith Holyoake to the other, and the opposition the venerable Walter Nash to both (he was greeted with standing ovations). I did not get along too well with the more obsessed protesters; I recall that veteran, Don Swan, reacting with great hostility to my opinion that Keith Holyoake was not actually an evil man. The very sight of Holyoake, he said, made him physically sick. I turned my teach-in speech into an essay for *Landfall* on 'Moralism and Foreign Policy'. Foreign policy should be an expression of national interest, I argued; Americans were not pursuing their interests but rather undertaking a pernicious moralistic crusade; we were defeating our own interests by joining it. Walter Nash told me that he agreed with this analysis, and (inconsistently?) that he had always been a moralist himself.

Vietnam continued to haunt the decade, but I devoted little further energy to the protest movement. I continued to hanker for greener and more British historical pastures, and applied unsuccessfully for a chair on the teaching side of the Australian National University, where British history was strong. I was not at this time accustomed to failure, and did not enjoy it. My recovery from this setback was accelerated by a wholly unexpected offer from the University of Alberta, to take up a year's visiting research professorship in the English department. I was a little disconcerted to find that I had been nominated on the strength of my standing as a poet, for I had written nothing for some years. Still, this was an offer which even a guilty ex-poet could hardly refuse – full family air fares (not, I think, that anyone expected the appointee and his wife to arrive with five children and return with six), a substantial tax-free grant and no set duties. It sounded, and indeed turned out to be, too good to be true.

I tried to justify my presence with a few appropriate activities. I offered a fortnightly seminar on New Zealand poetry; quite a few staff members turned up. It was a huge department; every university entrant had to take an English course and in my year there were 1,500 of them. Many staff members were novelists and poets who took creative writing courses; I was told that you could get a PhD by submitting a novel. On the staff was the eminent poet Dorothy Livesay, who summoned me to her apartment high in the pale blue Alberta sky to read and discuss my poems. I had feared something of the sort and had brought some with me to Canada; I managed to write a few more for the occasion. I was considered to be rather interestingly pre-modern.

But I spent most of my time on historical research and writing. I had, after returning from Oxford in 1967, written to Fabers about a book on English millennialism. They had offered a contract, which I accepted. In Edmonton, thanks to an excellent university library, I was able to extend the research and complete the book. However, by the time my typescript turned up, Fabers had decided to reduce their commitments by withdrawing from contracts; perhaps the hidden hand was again drawing me towards New Zealand history. Although, much later, Auckland University Press accepted the book and *Prophets and Millennialists* was published in 1978, a Faber imprint early in the 1970s might well have tempted me to continue with British history. But by the end of the decade, New Zealand history, in the shape of a projected book to be published by Oxford, had taken over.

On the first Sunday morning in that frozen place – the first snow of winter was falling on Edmonton as we arrived – my wife looked out of the window and saw the pitched roof of a church not far away. She went there; I followed later. It was a small United Church of Canada congregation of middle-class liberals and intellectuals for whom religion was considerably a matter of doing good, as I soon discovered, to youthful drug addicts and Americans escaping the Vietnam draft. I wondered if my own sons might eventually have found themselves fleeing north if we had gone to St Louis two years earlier. Without a great deal of thought about the matter on my part, paralysed perhaps by the sub-arctic winter, our long entanglement with Catholicism ended. For Dorothy it was going back to somewhere close to the place she had come from; for me, though it took some years for the process to be completed, it was moving towards a position for which I do not have a name.

All else in this problematic year fades before its major event – the birth, a few weeks before our return to New Zealand towards the end of 1970, of Matthew George, in the eyes of our small-family Canadian hosts an incomprehensible addition to an already over-quota brood. (The slogan PEOPLE ARE POLLUTION figured in the graffiti on building-site walls, together with runic inscriptions of a Tolkienish kind.) This was the only birth at which I assisted; the midwife, an English immigrant working in a lavish hospital built by the federal government for indigenous peoples but little used by them, told me firmly that I should have as much to do with the end as with the beginning.

This Edmonton interlude, so unexpected both in its occurrence and its consequences, saw the beginning of changes – in my personal life, in matters of religion and in my professional life – that took many years to work out. I left British history behind, and wrote no poetry for the best part of a decade, until a fresh disturbance shook me into it again. I returned to the city and the university which were to contain me for another dozen years. There was plenty to be done in the department, and outside the university, in the growth time of the 1970s. I went back to work as if my life depended upon it; from time to time I was ready to believe that it did.

Being in a university and in a position to make a few things happen was an exhilarating experience. There was money for growth and so the satisfaction of planning for growth. New staff were regularly appointed to the history department from England, America, Canada and Australia as well as New Zealand. Some stayed, some did not: this was still a sellers' market. But the successes were many – Alison Hanham in medieval history, Barrie Macdonald and Kerry Howe in Pacific history, Basil Poff in Indian history, Robin Gwynn in early modern history, Peter Lineham in modern English history, Margaret Tennant in New Zealand history – all added to the original foundation so capably laid down by John Owens and Warwick Tyler. I looked up and down the country and knew that as long as I was in a New Zealand university there was nowhere I would sooner be.

Massey University was still in the process of coming together. But whatever the problems as the old and the new, the sciences and the arts, the apparently pure and the patently applied settled down, research was an activity through which people could meet in mutual respect. The history department established itself in research and publication, and earned the respect of the university itself and of other history departments. Books, journal articles, conference papers and theses came in a steady flow. Massey was closer to the Wellington libraries and archives than any university other than Victoria; we cleared, as much as we could, Friday afternoons and Monday mornings to allow long weekends in the capital.

My part in this was small, limited to a handful of essays and papers in social welfare history. Even with delegation, an unavoidable number of administrative chores were in my care. They were onerous but, in an age in which staff assessment and student evaluation were hardly known, in which staff promotion was a reasonable expectation, in which a decent economy in the use of resources was sufficient accountability and, in a word, in which victories of the managerial ethos were in the future and administrators were still led by academics, their burden was bearable. Moreover, such duties could be believed in as a truly academic activity.

I count the administrative effort I made in these years to have been as valid as teaching, research and publication. Would senior university staff so cheerfully say that today? In the event, I left university work in 1983; I think I got out just in time, before the Indian summer ended.

CHAPTER NINE

A Time of Turning

The return to Palmerston North in 1970 had a feeling of uncertainty about it, an overtone of impermanence and a hint of impending change which persisted for more than a dozen years. The inner reality had altered but the outward and visible signs remained the same; there was the city, the university, the school and the house – an old house, full of a history I could only imagine. Later in the decade I began to write poems again; a number were centred upon this house and its runaway garden – an ancient magnolia shedding petals, a peacock screaming at night across the road, a thicket of bamboos where crowds of sparrows nested, bantams living at large in the trees, a barbecue as the sun went down and the day darkened, the brief bright lights of Guy Fawkes night, and the old house itself going quiet at night:

> Old house, you are close to your end,
> you do well to fall silent.

I collected them together in *Out of Season*, a volume which appeared in 1980, twenty years after my first; it remains an apt memorial to a time of stress and redirection, the beginning of a time of turning that has brought me, still slightly breathless, to the place where I am now.

I began to look for new meanings in personal living and historical activity. My professional life did not significantly alter; I continued to operate within the traditional structures of power, extending my activities outside the university. The centre of my life shifted steadily towards Wellington. In 1973, thanks to the election of a Labour government the previous year, I was appointed to the University Grants Committee – a political appointment which could not plausibly be attacked as such. For five years I went to Wellington for its regular two-day meetings; out-of-town members were put up at the James Cook hotel, the first and (thankfully) the last time I knew such soulless luxury. I was also recruited as a judge for the Book of the Year award; I began to concern myself with the politics though not yet with the practice of literature. There was, too, a quasi-official social science research group which wanted an historical perspective; one of its members referred to my contributions as 'the *déjà vu* file'. I had, outside my department and faculty, little opportunity and less appetite for the exercise of power, but I enjoyed being in a position to observe its manifestations and (often) unexpected consequences.

The history of social policy became my major professional interest; around this time there was a good deal of argument about the future of social security. I wrote an essay on the origins of the welfare state for *Social Welfare and New Zealand Society* in 1977, and shared a conference session on social policy history with Margaret Tennant, which led to publication in the *New Zealand Journal of History* in 1979. Her doctoral thesis on the old charitable aid system was a joy to supervise; the true rewards of the research supervisor come when it is unclear who is supervising whom. Many years later, while I was working for the DNZB, I was invited to write an historical survey for the Royal Commission on Social Policy; a lengthy essay was published in the Commission's four-volume April report in 1988. This proved to be my swansong in social policy history.

In these years, the early 1970s, my living and thinking were profoundly altered by the impact of feminist thought and by individual women. At that time, indeed, it was difficult not to be influenced by a body of theory and a programme of action which entailed a new way of looking at both women and men, and especially at the problematic character of their relationships, political, social and personal. The change these insights brought about in me was limited to the personal sphere; it never occurred to me to relinquish the pleasures and privileges conferred by the world of power. Does anyone ever do so, saints and martyrs aside?

I was not unprepared for this change. Virginia Woolf's *A Room of One's Own* and Simone de Beauvoir's *The Second Sex* had made an impression on me years before, when I had read them out of a fascination with Bloomsbury and a curiosity about existentialism. But those books, together with some random reading, and a good deal of listening to women, helped me to see more clearly (late in the day for such an unexceptional conclusion) the injustices and frustrations that women experience, and the ways in which they are likely to suffer from any effort to express an independent spirit.

The writings of Germaine Greer and Kate Millett opened up new possibilities; I readily accepted the conclusion that a freer life for women would also liberate men from damaging limitations. More closely related to my professional life, because it was historical and Australian, Anne Summers's *Damned Whores and God's Police* helped me to see another dimension in New Zealand history. At the same time individual women I came to know showed in their own lives how they had, often at great cost, rejected traditional social roles; my friendship and dialogue with women whom I can only call people of power prompted me to think again about history and society.

There is an irony here which, if it escaped me at the time, does not now – that such an encounter with feminism should go along with a persistent incapacity to live well within a relationship closer to home than any other. However, though not in that context, I learned a little of the ways in which it is possible to remain very much one's own person in relationship, even to become more one's own, and that in a good relationship power and position flow two ways. My long, difficult and enriching friendship with Lauris Edmond began about this time. She was making much the same journey but, just because she was a woman and one of my own age, a more arduous one. Men, it has often been remarked, have the advantage of being more or less expected to leave the straight and narrow and do not automatically lose position and standing when they do so. Our conversations ranged widely over the questions, both specific and general, posed by the changing positions of women and men in society.

With lasting consequences, I began to know Bridget Williams. Together we designed the *Oxford History of New Zealand*, the largest task either of us had embarked upon and one that neither would have been able to carry through without the other. At that time OUP was building up its local list; Bridget was recently back from England, and this was her first step in a commitment to New Zealand publishing. The idea for a new and comprehensive general history of New Zealand began with her perception that there was a need and a market for one. I realised that this was the way to go. No more short histories; if anything, we already had too many. It was time for a blockbuster. The plan was truly a shared insight; each of us realised, at about the same moment, that it should be 'a work of several hands', not of a single author. There was no one, it seemed obvious enough, ready and able to take on that task; I certainly was not. More, it should be as far as possible the work of the generation which had succeeded that of the old hands, Sinclair, Oliver *et al*. The unity of the book should be ensured by firm editorial design and management. Both in conception and execution, it was a joint project; we worked together upon it for five years.

Since the Sinclair/Oliver (unidentical) twins at the end of the 1950s, New Zealand history had come of age. It had become a full academic discipline, pursued in most universities from introductory undergraduate courses to postgraduate study. More research, it seemed certain, had been done from the mid 1950s to the mid 1970s than in the entire preceding century. At Auckland Keith Sinclair had founded the *New Zealand Journal of History* in 1967, the country's first academic history journal. The output of scholarly books had increased as historical publishing had moved away from the antiquarian to the monographic, and as commercial publishers (many of them with overseas head offices) and fledgling university presses raised their sights. A steady flow of theses, mostly for MA and some for doctorates, came from the university departments. There was a need to make this specialised work available to general readers as well as to students.

For, in addition to this academic expansion, the reading public for New Zealand history had grown. Bridget saw that the needs of the student and the informed general reader (often a former student) were much the same and could be served by the one publication. Happily, sales proved this to be a sound assessment. We determined to produce a history which would show New Zealand to New Zealanders and New Zealanders to themselves; most earlier general histories, beginning with William Pember Reeves, had been commissioned overseas to show New Zealand to the outside world – this I knew for I had written one of them.

A quarter of a century later, now that a radically different history has been endured, the *Oxford History* has an air of engaging innocence about it, reflecting the spirit of an age which had survived Vietnam and was yet to encounter the more sustained fury of the politics of race and religion. The *Oxford History* was to be, quite simply, a reliable one – 'reliable' was a word we were fond of – and one that could be read for both pleasure and instruction. This, once again, places it in the context of a vanished time; no one, subsequently, could have so thoroughly ignored the nagging reminders of uncertainty and relativity offered by post-modernism. But if those historiographical problems did not surface, more methodological ones did; should, for example, the book be organised chronologically or thematically? The upshot was a hybrid structure, one which would minimise the disadvantages of both. There would be four successive chronological sections; within each there were to be a number of thematic chapters, on politics, the economy, intellectual development, social structure, Maori history, race relations.

So we set about our task. A group of mainly university historians was invited to discuss the programme; the meeting was encouraging, once the notion that this should become an editorial rather than an advisory committee had been firmly, if gently, put down. Before long, chapters were allocated, boundary disputes settled, a timetable drawn up, and commissioning set in train. Most of the contributors were recruited from historians who had begun to make their mark in the 1960s and 1970s, and already had an impressive research and publication record. There were risks in that policy, but they were well worth taking: some chapters, especially on social, intellectual and Maori history, made the New Zealand past strikingly new, and did so with the vigour and enthusiasm of youth. This was especially the case – to pick a couple of winners from a strong field – with Ann Parsonson in Maori history and Peter Gibbons in intellectual history.

The intention informing the design was not, of course, limited to the laudable goal of presenting readers with the results of recent research. The book was to be an exploration of the way in which New Zealand had become a distinctive society in the period, of about two centuries, since the first contact between Maori and European. Many of those characteristics would be found in the ways in which those two peoples had interacted, in and out of conflict, and were continuing to interact. There was a good deal of new research and new thinking to be incorporated. That was not so much the case with social history and intellectual history, two other themes I wanted to emphasise. The kind of society which had evolved here, and the kind of thinking its emergence had prompted, had not been researched and pondered to nearly the same extent, but the relative paucity of firm results made it all the more important to ask thoughtful historians to try to fill the gap.

Maori history presented a few special problems. As far as I could see there were no Maori historians in a position to write for a publication of this kind; some consultation among Maori confirmed that conclusion. Not for the first time – but perhaps for the last without prompting adverse comment – the Maori history was written by Pakeha historians (and an anthropologist) and written admirably. No other general history had devoted so much space and so great a proportion of the whole to the Maori past.

The decision not to have a separate Maori chapter in the final section of the book (roughly from the Second World War on) had a more ideological character to it. I believed then that by the middle of the twentieth century Maori had become sufficiently integrated into the mainstream of New Zealand society for their history to be explored within the general categories of politics, economics, social structure and culture. This was, perhaps, a curious decision to make just a year or so after the Land March of 1975. The subsequent resurgence of Maori cultural activity, the abundance of ethnic identity statements and the rising tide of grievance, protest and demand make it unlikely that such a decision would be reached today. Nevertheless, I still consider it to be a not unreal way of looking at that topic. The distinctiveness of Maori experience is proclaimed, but (for the time being if not for much longer) its more concrete manifestations and aspirations are firmly integrated with the structures and institutions of established society – capitalist business enterprises, party political organisations, health and welfare systems, public media networks and the state bureaucracy. It is not easy to see how recent Maori history could be written as an entirely separate account within a general history, even in the twenty-first century.

Something of the same kind occurred with external affairs history – imperial, Commonwealth and foreign relations. I am less ready to concede here that my vision was significantly blurred in the 1970s; nevertheless, this is the point at which vision and execution most significantly diverged and where the law of unintended consequences had most effect. There was, certainly, an 'inwardness' about the original design; it seemed to me that politics, economics and ideas should be seen as dimensions and manifestations of an increasingly complex society. I had always been impatient with those elaborate studies of external relations and foreign policy which assume them to have a life of their own. Each writer, it was planned, would incorporate 'the external dimension' into the stuff of his or her chapter. That in fact is what happened in the second part, but in many other chapters (including the one I wrote myself) the external dimension of, say, politics, social development or ideas fell between the cracks. I can well understand the pressures which defeated the original prescription: there was just so much to say about domestic matters that the rest was relegated to the periphery at best, and for the most part beyond it.

Nor were any separate chapters devoted to women, for the same reason. Oddly perhaps, in the light of my interest in feminist thought, women did not feature as prominently as might have been expected. It had been noted earlier by feminist critics, with justified sharpness, that Sinclair's short history had one index reference to 'women' while mine had none at all. There are only nine women named in the index to the *Story of New Zealand*, all writers – alas for Kate Sheppard, Grace Neill, Elizabeth McCombs, Elizabeth Gunn (who had in fact inspected my head for lice) and Mabel Howard (for whom I had once voted). The *Oxford History* at least had a solid block of index entries under 'women', and the names of many individuals (with, however, too much of an inclination towards writers and artists at the expense of other callings).

In some measure thanks to its exclusions, the book has a unity, one difficult to describe except with words like mood, tone and spirit. This was an outcome, first, of editorial design and second, of editorial control. Most authors, predictably, wrote at excessive length; the first job was to get them down to something like their proper share of space. That required excisions, sometimes massive and mostly considerable. Many small and a few large additions were also needed to fill gaps; authors are likely to be idiosyncratic as well as leisurely. And (it should be said in hushed tones) there was a need from time to time for corrections: one author was at first indignant that there had been a careful check, before realising the outrageousness of the objection; another grudgingly, but not ungratefully, reflected that he had made that mistake in lectures for years; yet others accepted the corrections in a spirit of good cheer, as if that kind of inadequacy was to be expected from busy academics; a small minority, it must be noted, were impeccable.

The programme worked: a thick volume was published under the Clarendon Press imprint (unusual for a book initiated at the periphery of OUP's empire) in 1981, five years after its inception. The *Oxford History* was designed to provide an up-to-date body of information and interpretations that would help people to know themselves and their country better. Only readers and students can judge whether this has worked, and of these there have been many, leading to a revised edition in 1992, a book that remains in print ten years later.

I fled to London the moment the book was out. The Wellington launch had its troubles – cross-traffic from a test match at Athletic Park prevented the guest speaker, the former Labour leader Arnold Nordmeyer, from arriving at the National Museum until quite late. The guests grew restive and rebellious: Fred Page, not unexpectedly, told me that it was intolerable. But in London, things were more decorously done. The High Commissioner,

Les Gandar (a former chancellor of Massey), had an early copy sent by diplomatic pouch to be presented to the Queen at a dinner preceding her New Zealand tour. The launch itself, held a little later on the top floor of New Zealand House, was a more light-hearted affair. I shared the lift with the romance writer, Barbara Cartland, on her way to a celebrity function, and crouched under the brim of her immense cartwheel hat. Winnie Davin mistook the more glamorous Cartland event for ours and left the lift at the wrong floor; Dan gloomily wondered if she would ever be seen again. The place was full of expats; the doyen of them all, Ronald Syme, beamed genially if rather absently on the proceedings while toying with a white silk handkerchief. Dan Davin gave a splendid and generous speech. The High Commissioner had banned political activity but people moved steadily around the room distributing leaflets and a lapel badge for the anti-Springbok demonstration planned for the following day: this was 1981.

At the demonstration the police were nervy and numerous, thanks to the recent shooting of a London policewoman outside the Libyan embassy. We were not allowed to march or to assemble on the New Zealand House side of Haymarket, but packed the pavement on the opposite side. It was a hot day; John Thomson, once the editor of *Hilltop* and now of *Early Music*, the composer Robin Maconie and I drank a bottle of cool white wine in John's Ely House office and strolled a few blocks to the demonstration, wearing our NZERS AGAINST RACIST TOURS badges. My wife was not impressed by our little faraway show; she and Elizabeth had been marching regularly in Palmerston North. Hugh had followed the Springboks from match to match, at times in serious danger. He may be seen in the film *Patu*, white-faced, on the outer line of the human square that occupied the pitch at Hamilton and forced the match to be abandoned. Watching from London, we were startled to see New Zealand leading the six o'clock news – the police battling civilians in our familiar suburban streets.

I returned to writing poems during the 1970s in response to a complex set of stimuli – literary, historical and ideological, as well as personal. I had not previously tried to keep history and poetry entirely apart but I now found it useful to bring the two more closely together. After all, I reckoned, poetry arises from experience and a good deal of my experience is of the past. I had started to read poetry again and re-encountered some modern American poets I had not known well before, especially Robert Lowell and John Berryman.

Lowell was a profitable master. There was, I came to see, a way of doing poetry in which the personal and the public, the historical and the sociological, the intimate and the argumentative could jostle around together and, with luck, combine in an integrated utterance. The poems from this time were published in *Out of Season*. Some look to my domestic life; some to the social world around me; and a number to the history I was daily dealing with in other ways. Most resonate with a note of loss and portray the working out of an unpropitious destiny; many are flawed with that rather strained rhetoric I have seldom been able to eradicate. Today a few of them show up in anthologies and one of them – 'Parihaka' – in a glass case in an art gallery. That poem, and a couple of others on Maori–Pakeha themes, prefigure the anti-colonial impulse I took into the Dictionary of New Zealand Biography project and the more emphatic decolonising programme that informed my first transactions with the late twentieth century spirit of Waitangi.

In 1981, as well as seeing the *Oxford History* launched, I took a few months on leave in London and Cornwall. I was, if anything, more muddled and incapable than ever in my personal life; I recall one early morning, after a night with a friend, hurrying along a London street saying to myself: 'Whatever will I say when I get home?' 'Home' at that moment was a bedsit in Notting Hill, in a street where Katherine Mansfield had once lived. I might have concluded, though I already knew it, that I was not good at either expatriation or domestic alienation. I was supposedly doing research, and indeed I had a topic – the cultural and artistic expression of British imperialism in the 1920s and 1930s. So I spent many hours at the Victoria and Albert, more enjoyably among the curiosities on display than in the art history archives. I tried to penetrate the obscurities of the Public Record Office's new retrieval system and was saved from utter failure by the computer going down. I walked to Kew Gardens and there spent the rest of the splendid day walking amongst the lawns and flower beds, and lying on my back watching the jets stream overhead. I had a few poignant days in Cornwall, my last visit there, and tried to put something of my perplexity into a poem called 'Mordros', the name of a house close to the cove where, it seemed centuries not just decades before, Dorothy and I had spent some happy times as a young married couple.

Back in New Zealand, no more light-hearted than when I had left, I turned to a different kind of writing. Chiefly for the sake of the goodness of keeping on working together, I accepted Bridget Williams's proposal to write a short (but, of course, reliable) biography of James K. Baxter for her new firm, Port Nicholson Press. My initial response was 'Yes – but only as long as I don't have to spend too long in his company.' It was done in something like eighteen months, efficiently enough, not without a few ups and downs. Frank McKay, a very decent and kindly man though a shade troubled by the obligations of his priestly calling, had secured the designation 'the official biographer', a phrase he was fond of using when talking of himself in the third person. I felt reasonably justified in elbowing in; I had little respect for the way in which that magnificent but far from exemplary human being was being turned into a plaster-of-Paris saint – the one role which, to give him his due, he did not try to assume. After all, Jim, especially under the guise of Hemi, had made himself public property – any number could play.

The book we planned was not to be a blockbuster biography but a 'portrait' composed of closely integrated text and pictures. Gary Blackman was commissioned to photograph key Baxter scenes in Dunedin and thereabouts, with help from Kevin Cunningham. Bridget researched the illustrations and Lindsay Missen designed the book. In spite of our carefully declared intentions there was trouble along the way. While working in Dunedin at the Hocken, and interviewing Millicent Baxter, I received a phone call to tell me that Frank had taken his resentment to Jacquie Baxter. She, very understandably, did not want to be caught in the middle of a literary scrap: unless Frank and I could settle our differences she would withdraw permission to read the Hocken material. We did, a little later, sitting at an outside table in the sun at the Settlement in Wellington. I think he had realised, in the end, that the two books were to be quite different; in any case, his was still some time off.

From then on, Frank and I were good friends. His big book came out many years later and won an award. I was at the Government House ceremony at which he received it in a wheelchair, briefly out of the hospital; it was my last word with him. Two aspects of his book struck me not quite favourably. First, he gave very explicit information about Jim's love affairs – for example, naming the woman with whom he had the affair celebrated (if that is the word) in the sequence 'Words to Lay a Strong Ghost'; I had been told who she was and that she had become a married woman with a family – a situation I did not think it proper to disturb. Second, it seemed to me that Frank was less than satisfactory in his depiction of Baxter's later religious concerns – he flattened his hero into a cardboard cut-out of orthodoxy. But Baxter's free-wheeling mind had gone off into new directions – Buddhism, Pentecostalism, and into the kind of humanistic Catholicism he had learned from Eugene O'Sullivan in Auckland, in which he found great relief from the semi-Jansenism he had absorbed from the Marists.

This was my first and only effort at biography. Inevitably my main sources were Baxter's own writings, unpublished letters and other papers in the Hocken and the Turnbull libraries. I treated his *Collected Poems* as an extended autobiography; with a writer as inventive as he was and as prone to mythologise himself, this was source material to be handled with caution. You were, most of the time, not getting a record of a simple event or fact but of the story he made up about it. But I was less interested in his testimony as to what happened than in his expression of what he thought it meant. I do not know and no one, probably, ever will quite know what happened when he, say, fell in love; I think he tells us, clearly enough, how he felt at the time and especially how he felt when he looked back. I certainly did not take his word for everything; historians have a few tricks of the trade to test the reliability of evidence, whether it is in a poem or a newspaper cutting.

The book, the last I was to write for nearly ten years, was appropriately launched in Dunedin at the Hocken Library, in a space into which the lift opened directly. Early in the evening its doors opened and Jacquie Baxter brought in Millicent Baxter in a wheelchair; here were the two women who, through all the vicissitudes of his life, had been closest to him. I have that picture indelibly in my mind. This was in 1983; before that year was out I had, with a decisiveness which surprised me at the time and still does, gone in a new direction, both personal and professional.

CHAPTER TEN

A Crowded Portrait Gallery

After I had finished with Baxter – not that he has ceased to revisit me – I was without an occupation, apart from teaching and administration. And, for that matter, teaching was not going well; this I rightly took as an ominous sign. I was nearing the end of my fifties; I had, since reading one of those awful pop psychology books called *Passages*, been tempted to think in terms of decades and to trust that the next would be a better one. Though my fifties had, if anything, been more disturbed than my forties, I persevered in the hope that the 1980s would see things come right, or at least less wrong. Maybe that was the case; by my sixtieth birthday I was quite differently situated; I was in a new job in a different city and, weekends apart, I lived in a different place. This is a long way to and around the situation: briefly, in 1983 I went to Wellington to manage the Dictionary of New Zealand Biography project. Such a departure, to an extent from my home and my marriage and an occasion of pain and distress to others, could give rise to explanations which revolve around guilt and blame, and I will not pretend that they are not relevant. Nevertheless, I am glad that at this juncture in my life I was able to find the strength – but only just – to make a break which opened the way to a new and eventually a good place on which to stand.

I can see now, as one commonly does in looking for an explanation of a past event, that behind the shift lies both a long term trend and a precipitating event. There had been many intimations of disorder: drinking too much (flagon sherry giving way to the more seductive whisky), playing Patti Smith with the volume turned up while I typed in my outhouse workroom, ending arguments by taking a long, long walk, once in a while writing a poem in which I saw the house, the street and the city falling apart – these things, and much that hurt more, went on and on. So did life; I still took up my station by the frying pan each working morning and cooked eggs as the children went to school. But there was one activity in which life did not quite go on and that was teaching, so central a calling that I knew something was seriously amiss.

I had never enjoyed tutorials, and now I started to cut them short, even to cancel them. But lecturing, a fine old pedagogic practice I had always enjoyed, delivered an unmistakable signal. For years I had walked into lecture rooms with a few brief headings, and the words had flowed for fifty minutes; I found new implications in the notes as I went along. Quite without warning I found that I reached the end of my notes after twenty minutes. I had to leave the lecture room and retreat to my office in alarm and confusion, pursued by a solicitous elder student (whose goal was to become an Orthodox priest). That was daunting; in a thoroughly understandable way my – mind? spirit? self? system? – had said 'Enough'. How I staggered through to the end of the course I do not now recall. Perhaps it was nightmarish enough to be suppressed; probably I managed to rally my forces and do a minimal job.

My Wellington activities continued. The Historical Branch of the Department of Internal Affairs had invited me to join their advisory committee. It met rarely, but sprang into life when the National Library attempted to take over the biographical dictionary project which the branch (under Ian Wards as Chief Historian) had successfully proposed to government. I found myself at a meeting that was considering the question of the dictionary and its editorship. As the discussion went on, I realised that this could be a way out of my personal problems (well, half a way); a unique opportunity which I could not possibly reject. It was also a chance to do New Zealand history on a grand scale, but this aspiration did not take shape right away. During a break I rehearsed the idea with Erik Olssen and, when the meeting resumed, announced that I would take an interest in the position of editor.

I did; in August 1983 I found myself with an office on The Terrace and a bedsit on Oriental Parade. In that room, close to the foot of Grass Street where Lauris Edmond had her cliff-side house, I looked out over the harbour and the lights of the city and wrote many bad poems; why, I wondered, if this was a new life did it not seem much of a one? However, I more effectively planned the creation of a biographical dictionary. For a while there were only two of us; Jenny Barrett, whom I had known at the Oxford University Press, was my secretary. There was, at first, more need to think than to act; our lunches tended to be lengthy, convivial and thoughtful.

Before I left Massey I had had an informal lunchtime discussion with some sociology colleagues on the balcony of Wharerata, the venerable house accommodating the staff club. The history and sociology departments had always got on well, to the benefit of each. Most of the sociologists were of a democratic and liberal spirit, and some fervently believed in participatory procedures. How, I was asked, would I organise the Dictionary? I talked of working parties, consultation, staff conferences, expert advisers and so on. But who, one persisted, would ultimately decide who was In and who Out? I flannelled around a bit before I gave up. Well, in the end I will, I admitted. 'Christ,' came the rejoinder, 'you're worse than the bloody Pope.' Many times, thereafter, I was to wish that this had been the case.

The Dictionary was to be an official government 'sesquicentennial' project; in 1990 New Zealand would celebrate the 150th anniversary of ... just what never became clear. Certainly the country would observe the passage of a century and a half since 1840; that simple chronological certitude concealed a multitude of uncertainties and ambiguities. Some talked of a 'commemoration' rather than a celebration, but that left the question as open as before. This imprecision was beneficial; we had no fixed prescription, other than that of publishing a biographical dictionary.

There was no more than an occasional political rumble. Once I referred to the 'British annexation' of 1840; it was reported that the Prime Minister, Robert Muldoon, did not care for the phrase – annexation was what countries like Soviet Russia did in places like Afghanistan. However, neither the Prime Minister, nor our benign Minister of Internal Affairs, Allan Highet, nor any succeeding politician made the least attempt at interference. We were free to fix our own direction. There were only two requirements: the publication had to be recognisable as a national biographical dictionary and the first volume had to be published in 1990. I was told by Brian McLay, the department's benevolent deputy secretary, that if 1990 did not see the first volume I would not see 1991. It was an empty threat (and a wholly friendly one); in 1990 I would reach what was then the compulsory retiring age.

There had been a delay of two years between Cabinet's endorsement of the project and its effective beginning in 1984. Preparation time was cut to six years, less than similar projects in Australia and Canada had enjoyed. Nor was the initial financing at all adequate. Perhaps the heroic example of Alec McLintock, who had brought out the *Encyclopaedia of New Zealand* in 1966 with only a couple of research assistants, had set a bad precedent. Even those two eminent enemies, Keith Sinclair and Ian Wards, agreed (separately, of course) that a couple of research assistants would do. No one had the least notion of the number of staff or the range of skills needed; nor had I until I looked about me. It took no more than a glance in the direction of Canberra or Toronto to get a better picture.

The staff brought together in March 1984 – James Belich, Claudia Orange, Charlotte Macdonald – was an unusually (if not quite harmoniously) talented group. But it was no more than a nucleus; by 1990 staff numbers had climbed to over twenty, together with additional Maori translators and consultants. In the years between, much of my time was spent making regular applications to the Lottery Board for more money, successfully for the most part, thanks to the implicit threat that 1990 might not see the first volume published. I could not begin to estimate the overall cost; it was certainly huge. In Canberra I was told that the vice-chancellor of the Australian National University would call in at the Australian Dictionary of Biography office from time to time and say that he just wanted to take another look at the volume that had cost half a million dollars. Half a million! He was lucky.

To ensure that what money we had was well spent, my general notions had to be translated into specific objectives. I read a good deal about the history of collective biographies, noting especially the evolution of national from universal (that is, European) biographical compilations. I knew, too, that there had been collective biographies of a more specialised kind – Foxe's *Book of Martyrs* and numerous collections of the lives of the saints. Maybe, too, Aubrey's *Brief Lives* and Vasari's *Lives of the Painters* would figure in the genealogy. One conclusion was obvious and, for my purposes, useful: the conventional link between nationality and collective biography was a recent development, in many instances designed to legitimise the emergent nation states of the nineteenth century and the post-colonial nationalisms of the twentieth century. In the English-speaking world, the eponymous ancestor was Leslie Stephen's *Dictionary of National Biography*. How ineffably British it was to assume that there was no need for the word 'British' in the title – and, even into the twenty-first century, to include in the *New Dictionary of National Biography* people from countries that had long since freed themselves from the British Empire.

National biographies, especially the post-colonial kind, concentrate upon those people in whose lives the fledgling nations could discover and celebrate their essential character. Not that such a killjoy formula was exclusively followed; while the British had a fondness for highwaymen and dotty clergymen, the Australians could resist neither bushrangers nor cricketers. In general, the people who had, it was believed, made and shaped the nation dominated the selections. Little or nothing was heard of those who did not so obviously contribute to that historical destiny – indigenous peoples, women, ethnic minorities, eccentrics and characters, or ordinary people who simply 'stood for' whole areas of social experience. It would surely be possible to acknowledge such people as these, and their part in the making of their country, without turning traditional elitism totally on its head. New Zealand's biographical dictionary could be sub-elitist and post-nationalist and at the same time pay due respect to the expectations of the sponsor-state. If we were clever and careful, we could still raise a monument, but one to a wider-than-usual historical constituency.

That agenda would allow us to avoid the diversionary problem of 'national identity'. It was my belief – long held and still maintained – that New Zealanders should not be too anxious to characterise themselves as a nation. Any definition of 'New Zealandness' is likely to be contrived, prescriptive and exclusionary; it will almost certainly tell some New Zealanders that they are in reality not what they consider themselves to be. Or, if that outcome is to be avoided, the definition would have to include so much variety and contradiction that it would collapse under the weight it was called upon to bear. Far better simply to accept and reflect all that variety at the outset, and proceed on the assumption that New Zealand is essentially a place where many different kinds of people live: that it is, in fact, best thought of as a society rather than as a nation.

This was a modestly radical programme, but still a radical one. We confidently believed that we were going to make something new; we would mobilise regional, tribal and vocational communities up and down the country; we would deliberately seek out those kinds of people who had been marginalised in the past; we would utilise computer technology to put this into effect; if we had to, we would call into being the writers needed for the task. It was a complex programme and, while it fell down from time to time, it worked. We did make a new kind of biographical dictionary.

I visited Canberra and Toronto to see comparable projects in action. The *Dictionary of Canadian Biography*, in particular, was an object lesson. Its scholarly rigour set a standard to be striven for and its procedures could be adapted to computing. Its highly self-conscious nation-building ethos helped me, in a negative way, to formulate a distinctive goal for New Zealand. Canada was in many respects unlike New Zealand – a continental country, with a potentially separatist French-speaking enclave, with loosely attached western provinces and the constant cultural threat from its overmighty neighbour. All that made 'nation-building' a more understandable preoccupation than it could ever be in New Zealand; the Canadians were, it seemed to me, intent upon celebrating the nation-builders because they were seriously concerned that the building might fall apart. The *Australian*

Dictionary of Biography provided a more laconic and laid-back example of a nation-building programme.

The most extreme example of nationalism, at least by repute, had been a dictionary of Indian biography planned to celebrate the achievement of independence in 1947. Its main criterion for entry was said to be the contribution made to national independence; this effectively excluded all those British and other foreigners who had figured in modern Indian history. But it posed a further problem: many, probably most, of those qualifying on this basis were still alive. So the editors departed from the usual convention that only the dead should be admitted. I refrained from trying to check the story; it served me too well as I went around the country talking about what we were going to do. I encountered the opposite extreme in Dublin. There the Royal Irish Academy (annually, so I was told, the word 'royal' was debated and retained) was sponsoring a project which would take in the whole Irish diaspora and include such people as Ronald Reagan and John F. Kennedy.

In New Zealand I resumed my peripatetic life; I was constantly on the move, tiresomely travelling by bus on Friday nights and Sunday nights for weekends in Palmerston North, as well as visiting other centres. Not long after coming back I flew to Napier after a meeting in Gisborne and felt less than well while travelling by bus to Palmerston North. I took to my bed in the little room next to the kitchen, felt worse and worse, became delirious and collapsed into a coma, to wake up some days later in the public hospital. No one quite knew precisely what the illness was – some strain of pneumonia, or perhaps Legionnaire's disease, a complaint about which we heard much at the time, said to be associated with air travel. I understand that I almost died; that I did not is in some measure due to Claudia Orange, who visited Palmerston North and insisted (to the hospital) that I must be well treated and (to me, not that I remember this) that I had work to do. After about a month I was back in Wellington, shaky but still smoking and drinking, and working much as before.

Through these visits and from the working parties set up in many districts, I learned something about the ways in which New Zealanders thought of the relationship between their locality and the country as a whole. Auckland saw itself as too big to be ignored, Wellington as too important – in these places the project was initially greeted with a rather cool interest. In Christchurch there was a strong feeling that Canterbury must take steps to ensure that the province was accorded its due (and weighty) place. Dunedin put up a fusillade of nominations so that the southern capital and province might be seen in something of their former glory, and also to lay a basis for their own publication; it appeared later as *Southern People*. The smaller centres, with a less strident but still real conviction that there was a great past to be recaptured, were keen to nominate their favourite sons and, upon urging, daughters. Together with a handful of special-interest groups and consultants, these working parties and their devoted convenors grew into an effective and broadly based network of historians, archivists, librarians, art history specialists, scientists and genealogists.

As well as bringing the regions more emphatically into the picture, we proposed to improve upon the record of the Australian and Canadian dictionaries in dealing with women and indigenous peoples – a record which could at best be categorised as unthinking neglect. In Australia the first peoples had been more or less written out of the generally accepted historical record and there was no specialist working party – as, by comparison, there was for the armed forces. While I was in Canberra, the existence of Aborigines was seldom referred to – once I was told that it was hard enough to know what their names were, let alone what their lives had been like. I talked to the Canadian staff about the DNZB's Maori side; I was assured that nothing of the kind would be possible in Canada where there were more than fifty distinct native languages. I also became aware of a feeling among younger staff that in fact no effort had been made. I suspect that nationalistic preoccupations in both cases pushed such considerations aside. The New Zealand dictionary was, in comparison, lucky to have been set up in the 1980s. Whether or not the Canadian and Australian dictionaries, only twenty years older, could have been more prescient is a good question. But in the context of later twentieth century New Zealand, more representative goals were entirely acceptable and indeed obligatory; few felt inclined to challenge these parameters, which had the hearty endorsement of our official masters.

In New Zealand, Maori had always figured prominently in settler myth and legend; Scholefield, in his 1940 *Dictionary of New Zealand Biography*, had included a great number of Maori, almost all of whom were men who had been important to Pakeha, as helpful heroes, valiant foes and murderous scoundrels. Half a century on, and in response to a transformed climate of opinion, it became necessary as well as equitable to seek out people who were important in a Maori view of their past, whether or not they counted for anything in the Pakeha memory. Our aim was to assess their significance on that basis and recount their lives in that context. In the event, that goal proved elusive, but it was something to have gone even a little distance in that direction.

Ranginui Walker, a long-term supporter of the Dictionary project, remarked after the publication programme had been completed that the great thing about the DNZB was that we went out and asked Maori what they wanted – we did not tell them what they could have. This was especially true in the matter of whom they wanted to see in the book. Sometimes the asking led to a lengthy discussion before there was a full answer. There was a meeting in my office with three Ngati Porou, led by Api Mahuika: for the first volume a list of some eighteen names was tabled; after a couple of hours we had agreed upon six of them; in the end there were thirteen.

There was a good deal of face-to-face consultation with iwi. Sometimes it did not work at all; in these cases we simply had to use our best judgement; we were not going to leave people out just because we could not get agreement. Most of the work of this kind was done through a working party, mostly chaired with considerable brio by Tipene O'Regan. Its membership was quite wide across iwi and regions; many had a broad knowledge of Maori history. The meetings were bilingual; general exchanges were commonly in Maori. Once in a while I had to ask for a translation, either of a critical point or a good joke. Especially in the early stages, when everything waited to be done and no one was quite clear about the ways of doing it, hilarity and near-despair went hand in hand. Once a different sort of history brushed up against us. The Court of Appeal was just down Molesworth Street and the hearings of the Maori Council case – an action brought to prevent the Crown selling off state assets, especially land, before Maori claims had been heard – was under way. (We had given a little informal help to the cause in the form of advice and, in Claudia's case, an affidavit.) While the working party was deliberating on the Maori past, the door burst open and a group of elated Maori leaders entered, exclaiming 'We've won! We've won!' That was the end of business for the day; the present had taken over.

That the DNZB was widely, if not universally, accepted among Maori was due to the influence of two great men, John Rangihau and Wiremu Parker. Te Rangihau was a leader of unrivalled prestige among Maori; for a time he spoke in favour of the Dictionary at gatherings up and down the country and, having given it a good start, passed on to other concerns. Bill Parker, a man of great learning, was in the office almost daily; that was a richly educational experience for all of us. Once I asked him what it was like to have grown up wholly bilingual; many stories later I had been given an insight into his early life.

It would be wrong to give the impression that all was plain sailing, but the ship did, in the end, reach port. There were a hundred and sixty essays on Maori in the first volume, not far off a third of the whole number. Some had been written by Maori and more by Pakeha scholars and by DNZB staff members, with a good deal of family and tribal input and consultation. These Maori entries were then translated into te reo – 'translated' is not really the word, 'rewritten' would be closer to the mark – and the first Maori-language volume, *Ngā Tāngata Taumata Rau*, together with its four successor volumes, has become a taonga.

Again after examining the record of our Canadian and Australian contemporaries, we determined to make a significant increase in the proportion of entries on women. There had been a growth in women's studies in recent years; more important was the number of women who, committed to or influenced by feminist thought, were ready to work strenuously to enhance what we sometimes referred to as 'the representation of women'. Some were on the staff; others were members of a hard-working and deeply committed working party; regional and other specialist groups responded to what we might call the spirit of the times.

Many Maori and many women, as well as many obscure Pakeha males, were people who had achieved distinction within a sub-national milieu, such as a locality or a hapu; their lives had not been played out in a wider setting. In terms of region and of activity and occupation, the Dictionary was to be more representative than such compilations had commonly been. This programme could be thought of as historically democratising in intent and outcome, just as the participatory structure of working parties and networks could be seen, in some measure, as a democratisation of the process of doing history. The enterprise can be seen as a kind of deconstruction – an unpacking of the notions of 'public' and 'national' history into their smaller, more intimate, more personal components (though we were not inclined to record striking sexual revelations which, at least in the more distant past, have left little trace). It could not be entirely an exercise in retrospective democratic justice, thanks to the imperatives of the genre and of its provenance – the accepted character of such works and the expectations of the sponsoring government. Still, it could go a considerable distance in that direction by following the hunch that much of the meaning of the past was to be found in these places and at these levels, that patience and diligence would enable the people whose lives expressed that meaning to be brought into the light, and that the results would be at least as interesting as the doings of great white males. It would be interesting to see if indeed a 'national' monument could be erected on such dispersed and heterogeneous foundations. Leslie Stephen's great work had proceeded from and duly celebrated the class structure of nineteenth century English society; in New Zealand, it was quite certain, we were not at all like that and never had been. We would do better to attempt the construction of a monument in accordance with some reasonably informed guesses as to what we had been like.

Finding the people who would 'represent' colonial New Zealand and together constitute a crowded portrait gallery in print was a major research problem; finding the people who could and would write about them in accordance with these goals required further innovation. We could not simply recruit academic historians; there were not enough of them. In effect, we had to create writers. A host of people who had done little or nothing of this sort before, or had done so only within a limited local or professional context, were pressed into service. Many wrote like angels; those who did not wrote well enough to be edited into reasonable shape. A few writers were paid to do batches of 'unplaceables', and staff members also wrote a number of essays.

After many vicissitudes, at times of my own making, the first volume in English duly appeared in mid 1990, followed later in the year by its companion volume in Maori. The former sold so vigorously that a reprint had to be ordered immediately. Margaret Austin, then Minister of Internal Affairs and like her predecessors and her successors a good friend to the enterprise, found that her office had to deal with callers asking where they could get a copy. The output (as I had learned to name it) had been delivered, tall, chunky and handsome in a strong green wraparound cover, monumental enough for my masters to be satisfied and, so intricate are the twists and turns of hegemonic politics, more than satisfied with its sub-elitist contents. Here, I vaingloriously thought, was another nice little democratic first for New Zealand, a small successor to old age pensions and votes for women. Not everyone was happy. When the volume was to be launched in Christchurch (in a freezing Provincial Council chamber, for someone had forgotten to turn on the heating), I sidled up to a couple in a bookshop who were carefully inspecting a copy, hoping to hear ... well, any word of praise would do. One of them said to the other, 'It's *very* disappointing, isn't it?' and shut the book with a bang. I slunk away, consoling myself with the unkindly thought that if they were, as I decided they must be, descendants of the pastoral gentry, they were just the sort we set out to disappoint.

By the time the first volumes were published – also the time at which I retired from the position of general editor – a large and varied staff had been drawn into the enterprise. There were editors, researchers, writers, linguists, translators, administrators, all doing work which was new to them, unavoidably so, since nothing like it had been done in New Zealand before. There was, too, a publisher; under its managing director Bridget Williams, Allen and Unwin New Zealand won the publishing contract and formed a joint venture with the Department of Internal Affairs.

Jamie Belich was initially deputy editor and, before he migrated to Victoria University, designed the selection procedures. Claudia Orange succeeded him as deputy, then became associate editor, thanks to the greater share of responsibility she carried as publication deadlines approached. Her determination and unceasing vigilance, her management of an intricate process of research, editing and preparation of essays, and especially her capacity to participate in all aspects of the Maori side, had much to do with the successful outcome in 1990. Suitably, she followed me as general editor and together we received the Wattie 'Book of the Year' Award for Volume One in 1991.

Some people of strong character and force of personality worked for the Dictionary; notable among them was Miria Simpson, assistant editor (Taha Maori), renowned for a sharp temper and for her skills in the Maori language. She made a marked impression on the kind of Maori in which the essays in the first volume of *Ngā Tāngata Taumata Rau* were written; it is, I have been told, by her and by others, a pure classical Maori suitable for the nineteenth century people it is used to portray. She had a distinct suspicion of Pakeha, especially when they were engaged on Maori matters. Once, when I asked her about a forthcoming meeting with some prospective Maori participants, she replied, 'Of course, you will charm them.' It was not a compliment.

She was intent, however, upon furthering the education of the Dictionary's Pakeha people, and arranged for the chairman of the policy committee, Robin Williams, and me to go with her to the annual Coronation hui at Turangawaewae, a major Maori event spread over four days. We slept in one of the huge sleeping halls, on mattresses on the floor, with the instruments of the Ratana band packed into the spaces between. 'Slept' is not quite the word; much of the night was given over to speeches and argument. I ended up outside the hall in the small hours smoking my pipe, and here my education did take place, talking with other sleepless smokers and observing the dedication of the Kingitanga people – at 2, 3 and 4 a.m. they were working on the grounds cleaning up the mess left the day before by 2,000 or so people. The same devotion was shown by those working in the great dining hall to produce three promptly served and delicious meals a day for that multitude.

One evening we went with Miria to the neighbouring house of a young married couple. As we talked, it became clear that they had committed their lives and their resources to the Kingitanga and especially to the care of Turangawaewae. That was a moving experience, the more so for its being so understated. Again, and I am unsure why this incident is so clearly in my memory, a conversation with some elderly men in the Queen's house about walking sticks (there were many splendid ones on display) took us to a nearby bit of bush where young saplings were being tended, their tops progressively bent to shape the handles as they grew. The activity in one marquee puzzled me; a steady rise and fall of voices came from it throughout the day – a prolonged religious ceremony, perhaps? No, bingo. My best times, apart from smoking and chatting in the small hours, were spent watching the performances and talking with the old ladies proudly pointing out their mokopuna on the stage. We left a day early, worn out by lack of sleep and lack of English. For everything was in Maori, including the voices on an inescapable public address system; the only messages in English related to wrongly parked cars and lost children. It was, in every respect, an education.

Later, Miria took me to another great Kingitanga occasion, the opening of the new dining hall on the marae at Kawhia, a beautiful and bittersweet location for me, for at Kawhia Dorothy and the children and I had spent our last two family summer holidays. On the second occasion I took a volume of Robert Lowell's poems and some novels of Patrick White – summer reading, indeed.

This was an international event; the Queen, Dame Te Atairangikaahu, was host to the representatives and heads of independent states, Tonga, Samoa and the Cook Islands. She was of no lesser standing; she was indeed a monarch even if not quite a sovereign. The Kingitanga kuia were clothed in long black or purple gowns and the women in the Tongan entourage in gorgeous floral gowns and elaborate wide-brimmed hats. The King of Tonga sat in all his immensity in a bower made of green branches, for the sun was high and hot. We were sheltered in the Queen's house to observe the ceremonies in which we could have no part. Later the King of Tonga gave a long speech in which he idealised and praised the qualities of the Polynesians, a race he clearly believed to be superior. David Lange, the Prime Minister, charmed everybody, especially by adding, after he had put down his koha, 'Cash it quick, while there's something in the bank.'

I went to London to see the volume launched at New Zealand House; as soon as I got there and made contact with Allen and Unwin, I discovered that the firm had been absorbed by an even more multi multinational and that its New Zealand operation had been closed down. It was a rather muted celebration we had at New Zealand House, hosted by Bryce Harland, the High Commissioner. A new firm, Bridget Williams Books, took over much of the local Allen and Unwin list, and published the next two volumes of the *Dictionary*; the fourth was also brought out by Bridget Williams after she formed a brief alliance with Auckland University Press, the *Dictionary*'s current publishers.

Dorothy had died two years before the publication of the first volume. She was found to have cancer of the pancreas and died in 1988 after a few months of often severe suffering. I spent much of the time of her illness in Palmerston North; she was surprised and pleased at the number of people who came to see her. There was an ambiguous religious side to her dying; she was infuriated by a busy man who insisted on praying too much for forgiveness. But she was glad to receive communion; I did too, thinking that this was no time for theological niceties. She spent her last days at the Mercy hospital in Palmerston North. One day, after I had read her a passage from the epistle to the Romans, she fell asleep as I sat beside her bed working on Dictionary scripts. She gave a deep sigh. Soon after that the nun in charge entered, took one look and said to me: 'I think your wife has had her wish.' She had also, though no one else knew, had another wish answered a few days before – we had made our peace with the few words it takes when that is deeply wanted. She had drawn up her own order of service for her burial; we added to it the passage from Romans. Her coffin was carried by her five tall sons, and a slightly built Cambodian from the community which honoured her so highly for her help in their resettlement. Elizabeth and I followed her body out of the church. After the cremation I saw a group of Cambodians looking intently upwards at the tall chimney; they were waiting to see the smoke rise. I explained that a faint heat shimmer would have been all there was to be seen, and we went off to the gathering at the old house.

CHAPTER ELEVEN

Histories and Politics

I retired in 1990, not long after the first tall volume of the *Dictionary* had gone out into the world, for the most part a welcoming world. In my turn, I went out into an unanticipated vacuum; until a few old tasks returned and some new ones arrived, I was seriously disoriented. I had been showing up at work, to my office, my desk, my fellow workers, the copying machines and the telephones, for the best part of fifty years. My life, to much too great an extent, had been centred on the workplace and upon the salary and the non-salary benefits such privileged occupations as mine provide. For decades I had not had to trouble myself over such items as manilla folders, paper and envelopes, ballpoint and felt-tip pens, paper clips and bulldog clips, an inward and outward mail service and (of value because Wellington days are often cold and dull) heat and light. Never before had I thought about these subsidies; I felt a burst of sympathy for the self-employed whose ranks I was soon to join.

Even the geography had changed. I had by now purchased a small Mount Victoria flat, far across town from the office in Molesworth Street where I had shopped, bought papers, banked, had my hair cut, taken my prescriptions to the chemist and my back to the physiotherapist. I had some letters to write and managed to equip myself with paper and envelopes; I set off to the nearby post office to buy some stamps. It was, I remembered, on Cambridge Terrace, near Courtenay Place. The tall building was still there, but it was not a post office. I made enquiries and learned that the nearest post shop (not office) was several blocks further on, in Manners Street. I trudged off and eventually posted the letters, which by now I rather regretted having written. These are, perhaps, small matters, but the dislocation of retirement is not in the least trivial.

From this predicament, and from the solutions offered by bowling clubs, good works and leisurely supermarket shopping, I was rescued by Claudia Orange, my successor as general editor of the Dictionary. She offered me part-time editorial work, and I returned to a desk in a corner of an office and to a kind of quality-control function, with a hand on each essay as it passed through the system. Here was an activity I enjoyed – editing historical writing and, in this case, editing the work of other editors. I went on doing this throughout the 1990s.

While this job provided continuity, an unexpected invitation from the Waitangi Tribunal brought about a refreshing, if at times an exhausting, change of occupation. Upon Claudia's suggestion, I was offered a commission to write a book for the Tribunal's fifteenth anniversary. I was in a general sense aware of the Tribunal's activities and thought well of its objectives; I accepted, out of an interest in the topic and with some pleasure at the prospect of a challenging assignment. This was the beginning of my lengthy and ambiguous involvement in a new kind of history, a history inextricably caught up in politics.

Although many surprises were in store, I was not entirely unprepared for this activity. Many of the people with whom I had mixed on the Maori side of DNZB work were also engaged in claims and negotiations; the chair of the Maori working party, Tipene O'Regan, was the chief Ngai Tahu negotiator, and Robert Mahuta, with whom we did business on Kingitanga representation, was the chief negotiator for Tainui. In a more general way, the Dictionary's effort to raise the historical profile of Maori was a modestly decolonising venture – to an extent, at least, the descendants of the colonised were able to write about the tipuna who had first encountered the colonisers.

From teaching and writing New Zealand history, I already respected many of the leaders who had responded to the impact of colonisation, at times by resistance and at times by adjustment. The Maori prophets made a deep appeal – Te Kooti Arikirangi, Te Whiti o Rongomai, Rua Kenana and T. W. Ratana. At Ratana village I noticed that the only carved building housed the crutches, trusses and spectacles discarded by those the prophet had cured. Near Gisborne I spent hours in the painted house, Rongopai, erected by Te Kooti's followers to welcome him back to Turanganui. East Coast history also led me to admire the succession of Ngati Porou leaders, from Rapata Wahawaha to Apirana Ngata, who had dealt with the Pakeha in another manner, by putting them (as they hoped) to use.

This was the intellectual equipment I brought first to the Dictionary and then to the Waitangi Tribunal. *Claims to the Waitangi Tribunal* was a short book, quickly researched and written; I had no time to attend to the earlier history of Maori efforts to obtain redress from the Crown, to the worldwide context of indigenous rights, or to the diversity of opinion – approval and discontent – within which the Tribunal did its work. This was to be a summary of the claims the Tribunal had dealt with, its jurisprudence, especially the derivation of 'principles' from the text of the Treaty, the historical reconstructions evaluated in the light of these principles, the findings as to the ways in which the Crown had not fulfilled its obligations, and the (distinctly meagre) responses of government to its recommendations for redress.

As I wrote, I developed a strong respect for the imaginative vision and intellectual subtlety of the man everyone knew – in spite of the anonymity of the reports – to have invigorated the Tribunal and fashioned a new evaluation of the New Zealand past, its second chairman E. T. Durie. I did not write the book as an advocate; nevertheless, it was clear enough that I supported the process I was describing. Ranginui Walker, who had done so much for the Dictionary, gave the book a gentle review concluding that it was so dispassionate as to be bloodless. From where he stood, a much more engaged position, this was fair enough. His comments could have helped me to realise (but at the time did not) that for most of those who practised it in this context, history was not above the battle.

This commission was followed by an invitation from the Crown Forestry Rental Trust to report on the submissions made for and against the Muriwhenua claim; the Trust was financing the claim, which had been made by a runanga representing the five tribes and led by Matiu Rata, who had been Minister of Maori Affairs when the Tribunal was set up in 1975. So began my bit part in the drama of that great claim, for me an adventure into a strange country and for claimants and Crown alike a prolonged experience of frustration; the Tribunal took seven years to report on the claim, and after another five it still awaits settlement. The Trust asked me to read the evidence presented by the claimants and to say if I thought a sufficient case had been made against the Crown; in the language of the trade, did it show that the Crown was in breach of the Treaty of Waitangi through acts and omissions prejudicial to Maori? At first I doubted that it did; I was generally unimpressed by the case made here for the tuku whenua position – that is, the argument that, if land transactions were closely examined, it would be shown that Muriwhenua people did not sell land at all, but merely allowed settlers to use it in the expectation of reciprocal advantage. That, it seemed to me, had not been shown to be the case in the evidence brought before the Tribunal. Thus the Crown could not be said to have wronged the claimants on these grounds.

However, I believed that the claim could be securely based on evidence showing that the Crown's massive land acquisitions, often effected by dubious and at times fraudulent means, had brought about the dispossession and impoverishment of Muriwhenua Maori. This was clearly contrary to the Treaty promise of protection for Maori; and it was an obvious injustice. I developed an argument that the Crown – whether out of malice, carelessness or incomprehension was beside the point – had persistently acted against the interests of the claimant tribes by depriving them of their main means of support. At the same time I tried to persuade the claimants that relying upon the tuku whenua argument – that the Crown was in breach of the Treaty because it failed to recognise that Muriwhenua Maori had never in fact sold land – would not convince what I mistakenly believed to be an empirically minded Tribunal.

I worked closely with John Koning, a Trust historian; our function was to report on the Trust's assessment of the progress and prospects of the claim. At a meeting in Kaitaia he and I were vigorously challenged before we were allowed to speak – what were these representatives of the Crown doing here? It took a little talking to establish that the word 'Crown' in the name of the Trust did not mean the same as it did in, say, Crown Law Office but referred simply to the fact that these were 'Crown' forests. We were not, in any respect, speaking on behalf of the state. After we had talked, a youngish man replied at some length, thanking me courteously for a sound 'Treaty of Waitangi' analysis. I soon understood, with a rather innocent astonishment, that this was a criticism, implying rejection of that way of dealing with the demands of Muriwhenua Maori. I realised that, for those committed to the cause of Maori sovereignty, the business of claims and settlements, the Treaty itself and the Tribunal could be seen as obstacles in the path of achieving a larger goal – sovereignty, not compensation.

Early in 1994 at Pukepoto John and I made a joint submission supporting the Muriwhenua claim to the Tribunal; I outlined a pragmatic argument, based on the cumulative effect of Crown land purchasing policy and its damaging results for Maori. I promoted this argument in meetings with the claimants and in a few private conversations. At one meeting Rima Edwards, the claim committee chairman, firmly stated that nothing would be allowed to imperil the integrity of the claim; I knew this to mean that the tuku whenua position would remain at its centre.

It was from the Pukepoto hearing that I recall some of the special pleasures that participation in a claim can bring – not only the euphoria of having enlisted on the side of historic change but also the sociability of living and working with Maori. A number of people involved in the claim, Tribunal members, Trust personnel, claimant counsel and expert witnesses, shared a wonderful dinner at the De Surville hotel, of flounder caught that day and an excellent selection of wines. Manu Bennett, a member of the Tribunal known simply as 'the Bishop', regaled us with tales of his childhood as he ate the sweet meat from the flounder heads, saying that this was all he was allowed as a boy. Later, when my evidence was finished,

I sat in the meeting house, looking and, as far as I could with no Maori, listening. Mat Rata moved steadily about, constantly talking to this one and that (I was one of them) about the claim and his hopes for the benefits compensation would bring.

The Tribunal held two final hearings on the Muriwhenua claim in Auckland. At the first I was cross-examined by the Crown counsel, an experience that convinced me that this was no way of trying to arrive at the truth of the matter (I began to suspect, indeed, that this might not be the objective). The same lawyer presented the Crown's closing submissions at the second hearing; every important item in the claim was vehemently, even harshly, rejected. This was, not surprisingly, distressing for the claimants. (John Koning and I had attended the second hearing, and met with the claimants afterwards.) Muriwhenua Maori, like many in the north, had from the very beginning welcomed the newcomers, including the agents of the Crown who came to acquire land and had encouraged them to expect to benefit from the relationship. If there ever had been any hope of reciprocal advantage, here it was without a doubt repudiated. It was still, in spite of all the changes that had taken place, a case of winner takes all, and the winner was the Crown.

I attended a few more meetings after this but withdrew when it became apparent that I was not acceptable to all the claimants. After the Crown's closing submissions and after Mat Rata's death, the runanga suffered from defections as some participants went their own way. This experience of watching the disintegration of the Muriwhenua claim inevitably made me question the efficacy of the process. For, in spite of the hostility of Crown counsel, the claim appeared to have every prospect of success, if the claimants had completed negotiations with the government after the Tribunal had reported. If ever there was a Maori population that needed a sizeable cash injection, it was the one in the far north. The government was widely thought to want to complete a settlement which would have that result. But everyone knew that there would be no settlement without a clearly mandated authority to manage it.

I began to doubt, and the doubts have deepened with the years, the capacity of this and other strategies to bring about anything that could properly be regarded as decolonisation in such a thoroughly colonised society. But my commitment to the idea of redress for past injustice remained intact, and was rekindled in 1995 by the publication of the *Crown Proposals for the Settlement of Treaty of Waitangi Claims* – the proposal known as the 'fiscal envelope', by which the total compensation bill would be restricted to one billion dollars. Vehement Maori protest greeted this policy. For my part, I was especially hostile to the government's intention, as set out in this publication, of settling only those claims which arose from either breach of contract (as in the Ngai Tahu claim) or the unjust confiscation of land (as with Tainui and the Taranaki and Bay of Plenty tribes). With most other historians, I knew that confiscation, unjust and harmful as it was, had not inflicted as much damage upon Maori as the steady, indiscriminate and massive purchasing of land by the Crown from the mid nineteenth to the early twentieth century. The critical point was that the government had, in this statement, accepted the notion that perfectly legal acts of state (that is, the legislation effecting confiscation) could be unjust and so constitute a 'Treaty breach'. I argued that the same conjunction of legality and injustice, upon an even larger scale, could be seen in the Crown's land purchasing, both as a monopolistic buyer and later as a facilitator of private purchasing.

My argument was made in an article published in *New Zealand Books*; I went on to criticise the government for failing to pay any attention to another matter which I believed to be central to the issue of grievance and redress. The claims business, I contended, was about a good deal more than compensation. Maori were, I asserted, primarily concerned with power. Today I would hesitate to announce so brashly that I know what Maori want. Still, it seems to me not an unreasonable proposition. It is, surely, clear that for some Maori economic power, to which Treaty settlements may contribute, will lead to tribal autonomy and independence. Others, it also seems obvious, seek power through political institutions and administrative agencies. Many look to the acquisition of power through constitutional reform; some, even, through a separate polity. Whatever the form it takes, power is at the heart of the matter. I think it likely that the stirring of 'one nation one law' demands among Pakeha arises from this realisation.

Later in the same year I criticised a significant historical statement which the Crown proposed to make in the preamble to the Act providing for the settlement of the Tainui claim. The preamble was in effect a recital of the ways in which the Crown had acted wrongly to the Kingitanga through confiscation. There could, of course, be no quarrel with the statement that confiscation was wrong; however, the preamble asserted that no confiscated land had been returned to people who had fought for the Kingitanga. Readily accessible parliamentary papers of the 1870s stated that a good deal had been returned; I pointed this out to the Crown Law Office and the wording was changed slightly to say that land was 'generally not' returned to Kingitanga supporters. This was mere fudging but it stayed in place. I published a brief account of these exchanges in *New Zealand Books*. Later, I gathered that these criticisms had been kept in mind when subsequent settlement statements were being drafted.

This episode reminded me that those who have, for one reason or another, committed themselves in advance to a particular position may, and probably will, take a rather casual attitude to evidence. That lesson was repeated when, in 1997, the Tribunal brought down its report on the Muriwhenua claim. It found that there had been no genuine land sales in the period up to the 1860s and made this the main item in its indictment of the Crown – the very position I had confidently told the claimants the Tribunal was not likely to accept. I published a dissent which, for all its brevity, has had more public impact than anything else I have written. After I had been, quite incorrectly, described by a journalist in the *Sunday Times* as a 'fierce critic' of the Tribunal, I accepted an invitation from the *New Zealand Herald* to write an even briefer summary. I did, beginning by emphasising my support for the claim.

The Tribunal's finding, I argued, went a long way further than the evidence before it would allow – that evidence was too scanty, ambiguous and opaque to support any firm conclusion on the matter. Nevertheless, the Tribunal had concluded, very emphatically, that in doing land deals with settlers Muriwhenua Maori intended to grant no more than use rights and accordingly retained their right of ownership. This conclusion was based, apart from some items of linguistic evidence which were seriously contested, upon the present-day Muriwhenua belief that this was so and upon comparisons with other Pacific societies. Certainly these considerations were enough to justify the formulation of a hypothesis to be investigated further. On their own, they were not enough, so I believed, to establish a firm conclusion either way.

The position the Tribunal favoured related to a series of land transactions in this district beginning in the 1830s; of the evidence presented, not much bore directly upon these deals, and most of it was open to more than one interpretation. Had all this been going on in a learned journal, it would have been the occasion for a useful discussion, concluding with a call for further research. But it was not; it was conducted in a series of confrontational hearings and ended in an emphatic 'finding' in a report to government on the ways in which the Crown had been guilty of breaching the Treaty. To find, as the Tribunal did, that the Crown was in breach of the Treaty because it did not recognise and act upon an intention on the part of Maori to retain ownership in land which they might appear to have sold went so far beyond the evidence that it became an act of faith.

The pity of it all was that the claim did not – at least as far as I could see – require such hypothetical (and fragile) support. And indeed, as a kind of second-string argument, the report did advance a case based upon the deleterious socio-economic consequences of massive land purchases by the Crown. Of course I agreed with those aspects of the report; I had argued along these lines in evidence. I did not in the least dissent from the conclusion that Muriwhenua Maori had suffered at the hands of the Crown and should be compensated. Some will say, perhaps, 'Well, what does it matter how you get to that conclusion as long as you get there?' The only answer I know has something to do with truth and with the ways of reaching it.

This review made me few friends (except on the anti-Tribunal side, where I would prefer not to find them), though some among the claimants assured me of their friendship as well as their disagreement. Years later I was still being accused of 'breaking ranks' – that is, of not maintaining solidarity as a claimant witness. This poses a problem: what is a professional historian, even one who is part of the process, to do when he believes that a significant methodological error has been made by a powerful and respected Tribunal? Where does his primary loyalty lie – with the agency that retained his services or with the principles of his trade? I was, in fact, only ambiguously a claimant witness; the Tribunal's report identified me as an 'independent expert witness' when it cited my submission in support of other conclusions. But even had I been unambiguously a claimant witness, should I have kept silent?

Even while answering 'No', I know that it is a real problem, or should be, for those engaged upon this sort of history. There appears to be a convention that the participants in the process should abstain from public comment – even after the Tribunal's report upon a claim has been published, as in the Muriwhenua case. However, the Tribunal is not a court but a commission of inquiry; its findings are published in lengthy reports, and the greater part of its proceedings are held in public places – halls, meeting houses and court-rooms. Members of the public may attend and often do. In the case of the Hauraki claim, with which I was also involved, this time unambiguously as a claimant witness, my evidence (as well as that of others) has been published by the claimants prior to the conclusion of the hearing. So I feel free to discuss it here, without making any comment upon the claim itself or any prediction as to its outcome.

As my involvement with Muriwhenua faded away, I was recruited into a research team working for the Hauraki Maori Trust Board. For this claim the Tribunal, seeking to rectify the drip-feeding (sometimes flood-feeding) of evidence characteristic of the Muriwhenua hearings, had introduced a 'casebook' approach; all evidence was to be submitted by claimants before hearings began. It was, but as the casebook consisted of a dozen volumes, some very large, brevity and concision were not among the gains of the new approach. Still, it avoided the assertion and counter-assertion of the Muriwhenua hearings, with Crown and claimants engaged in a dialogue in which every utterance filled a small (or not so small) book. But the tedium persisted. Surely no one outside the system would believe that expert witnesses standing for hours reading whole books out loud is an efficient way of doing history, or indeed law?

There was an element of informality about the Muriwhenua claim – everyone talked with everyone. The Hauraki campaign was both more orderly and less sociable. The research team was almost wholly made up of Pakeha academics and we hardly ever met the claimants. My job, as it had been in part for the Muriwhenua claim, was the 'social impact' report. By asking for such reports the Tribunal required historians to deal with a difficult methodological problem – what is the causative connection between the loss of land and resources and the deprivation shown by high rates of sickness and death? I was regularly asked the question: 'Yes, but what is the nexus?' I was never able to give a simple answer for it was not a simple question. There are demographic techniques for establishing a correlation (and it is no more than that) between economic change and social deprivation, but I had neither the data nor the methodology for that. I could only ask a rhetorical question: given these two phenomena, resource loss and impoverishment, is it reasonable to suppose that there is no connection between them? The former brings about and the latter arises from a low standard of living. That persistent and widespread deprivation is wholly a matter of individuals choosing to be feckless and improvident, as 'dry' economists would no doubt contend today about ill health in, say, south Auckland, is patently improbable.

Even so, it remains a tricky question; individual choice (as the Tribunal has constantly pointed out in considering the activity of Crown agents) cannot be dismissed out of hand. Maori chose to sell most of the land, didn't they? and to misuse what they had left? and to spend what money they received upon alcohol, poor food and excessive hospitality? So runs the rejoinder of blinkered individualists. That dogmatism cannot be met with a simple denial that anything of the kind had taken place, because it quite obviously had. To show that such an account is essentially superficial and inadequate as a general explanation, the historian has to – well, this one had to – enter a discussion that turns upon the circumstances which may limit the scope for free choice and make individual motivation a matter of limited consequence. Men choose, as Marx said, but they do not choose freely. I attempted to cover these positions in my report and read it as a claimant witness.

While I was preparing my submission for the Hauraki claim, I was beginning to entertain doubts about the kind of history which this process required, especially the occupational obligation to find the Crown always in the wrong. The nineteenth century state ('the Crown') did not invariably sit idly by and blandly observe the decline of the Maori people, nor did it justify a lack of concern by pointing to the 'inevitability' of their extinction, as is commonly supposed. On the contrary, it did quite a bit for Maori health and rather more for Maori education – certainly that was indicated by the Hauraki example. While it would be difficult, perhaps impossible, to compare what the state did for Maori with what it did for Pakeha, in fact not a great deal was done for either and certainly nothing of the twentieth century 'social security' kind – an anachronistic model which the Tribunal has had some difficulty in getting out of its head.

Reflection on the nature rather than just the morality of the New Zealand colonial experience led me to realise – all over again, for it came out of my early training – that one had to pay heed to what was and what was not feasible in a given historical context, before charging past agencies (in this instance the state) with a failure to do things which, in those circumstances, it could not have thought of doing and could not feasibly have undertaken. So, in my Hauraki submission, I inserted a brief discussion of this problem, and tried to assess state action within the boundaries of what was reasonable and plausible to expect in a nineteenth century context. The outcome was still an argument that the Crown had not done as much as it could and should have done, but it conceded that the Crown had done quite a bit in health and education. Alas for good historical intentions; after I had testified, I was told that my moderate approach would be serviceable in reassuring the more conservative members of the Tribunal.

The hearing at which I presented these arguments was held on the marae near Paeroa in September 1999. I had by then been engaged in the claims process for nearly a decade. Apart from some short-term commissions from the Office of Treaty Settlements, my participation has since been limited to reflecting on my experience and upon the kind of history that arises out of that process.

The quest for 'reparative justice' (a phrase I owe to Andrew Sharp) is a striking historical phenomenon. Uniquely, perhaps, it allows historians to play a supporting role in a major historical drama as it is unfolding. Imperialism and colonisation permeate the entire course of human history. They have been, however, a characteristic of 'western' (European and American) history for the last four centuries. In the twentieth century imperial became post-imperial history, marked by decolonisation as the colonised inherited the power systems of the colonisers, by reverse imperialism as people from the peripheries moved into the metropolis, and – in a limited number of countries of which New Zealand is one – by programmes of reparation for the injustices inflicted upon the colonised. This phase is confined mainly to a handful of ex-settlement colonies: Canada, Australia and New Zealand, where the British legal tradition persists, and America, where the legal tradition has the same common law roots.

In these countries, especially among their governing elites, there has been a substantial if incomplete acceptance of the propriety of righting the wrongs done to indigenous peoples. Within that general position there is ample room for debate. To what extent were these injustices unavoidable aspects of colonisation? If they were, can specific agencies (for example, the state) be held responsible? How far should, or can, the effort at rectifying them go? By what right, if any, do the successors of the settlers continue to live (and rule) in these countries? Should reparation go beyond the straightforward matter of apologies and money into the redistribution of political power? Is it, and this is the basic question, realistic to act on the assumption that something can really be done to rectify history?

These questions seldom attract the Tribunal's attention; typically, it exhibits no hesitation in finding the relevant actions of the Crown to have been unjust and unjustifiable. Even so, its findings do show an element of ambiguity; they exist uncomfortably in the space between an appeal to the highest kind of supra-historical justice and the meagre recommendations it must make in the light of current political practicalities. The grounds for action which it upholds have been vehemently anti-colonialist; the actions it proposes, or asks government to negotiate, leave intact the power structure of a colonised country. This is not a condemnation of the claims process and the Tribunal's function. Rather, it is a sympathetic evaluation of the limits to its effectiveness. And, in a way, it is an exploration of historical irony, a suggestion that the effort to rectify the course of history may end up by confirming it.

I find it a paradox, more apparent than real, to share these reservations with radicals whose goals I do not believe can ever be achieved. It is not difficult to respect the cogency of a radical Maori assessment of both the Treaty and the Tribunal as colonialist stratagems. The Tribunal is indeed a means by which 'the settler state' ensures its continued dominance by paying premiums on a political insurance policy, though it is also more than that. Are would-be decolonisers running the risk of being the agents of a new colonialism, of a more paternalistic and sophisticated kind, but still a system of Pakeha power, renewed and reinforced by 'a show of justice'?

Given that the claims process has such an interesting and paradoxical historical context, it is surprising that few academic historians pay any attention to it. Those in university history departments who have participated can be numbered on the fingers of one hand. The *New Zealand Journal of History* has given it scant attention; Tribunal reports are massively historical but the *Journal* has reviewed only one of them. The legalistic demand for simple (and often simple-minded) answers has been too little tempered by academic caution and balance. It is both remarkable and serious that there has been very little public academic discussion of the Tribunal's historical analyses. As a result, the major context in which politics and history intersect in New Zealand lacks the benefit of intellectual debate.

While this context presents problems which I cannot solve and ambiguities I cannot eliminate, I have spent some time trying to understand them. Part of that process is an attempt to identify some of the historical pitfalls the protagonists, on both sides, are apt to stumble into. Another and a more important part is to attempt an analysis of what happens to history when it is pressed so rigorously into the service of a political process designed to achieve practical results. That analysis must begin with an acknowledgement that it is neither surprising nor improper that history and politics should go along together. It is not a matter of saying that this should not happen but of giving the results of the interaction the benefit of a stringently academic critique. It is bad for both the politics and the history if they are allowed to interact in a critical vacuum.

This was the intention behind a lengthy essay I published in 2001, in *Histories, Power and Loss*, called 'The future behind us: the Waitangi Tribunal's retrospective utopia'. I set out to answer the question 'what kind of history has been written by the Tribunal?' by examining two important reports of the 1990s, on the Muriwhenua and Taranaki claims. I concluded that in these reports it was not academic history at all but a history shaped by current political aspirations for a future in which Maori and Pakeha would share power. My quarrel was not with that as a present goal, but with the attempt to show that a New Zealand with something of that character had been a real possibility at the country's foundation and had been destroyed by the Crown's refusal to implement a form of colonisation from which the colonised would benefit and which they would, in good measure, control. The Crown had, so this argument went, promised in the Treaty to respect Maori autonomy; this it had, instead, destroyed. The proposition that colonisation could conceivably be conducted in the interests of the colonised is an unlikely one. The suggestion that the Crown could have pursued such a policy after 1840 earns, so it seems to me, the term 'retrospective utopia'.

I knew, of course, that the history to be found in the Tribunal's reports was an extreme instance of the political dimension to be found in all historical activity. That realisation, however, made it all the more important to identify the politics behind the history and to be alive to the possibility of distortion. I recalled Eric Hobsbawm's dictum that 'it is essential for historians to defend the foundation of their discipline: the supremacy of evidence.' I did not believe – and do not – that politics has no place in history, but rather that its place must be kept under careful scrutiny.

It was for reasons of this kind, though not so carefully thought through then as since, that on a few occasions I raised some critical questions about some of the history produced in this milieu. In the event, I did provoke a few responses. I submitted my reflections on the *Crown Proposals* to a government agency which had invited comment from the public; a number of quotations found their way into the subsequent report. My remonstrance to the Crown Law Office on the Tainui preamble did lead to a slight amendment to the Act.

I had only informal responses to my criticism of some of the Tribunal's findings in the Muriwhenua report. I heard on the grapevine a complaint that I should have said these things first of all to the claimants; the essay contained the information that I had done so. A more serious comment was made later, still informally: it was thought, I was told, that my critique had helped to persuade the government to reduce greatly the level of compensation considered due to Muriwhenua. I doubt if government policy gets made in a manner so flattering to historians. But that is not the point at issue here. My concern is that an argument had been met not by an effort to show that it was wrong but by an assertion that it would cost the claimants money. Politics, which up to that point coexisted with history (for, after all, the Tribunal had made an *historical* argument in its report), had swallowed up its partner. There was no history left in the contest but simply a contention that an argument had bad financial consequences. That is the end of dialogue between history and politics.

Why, indeed, should people concerned with promoting social justice in the present be troubled by the possibility of getting a few things wrong about the past? It is a good question and there is probably no answer likely to satisfy those whose focus is overwhelmingly on the present. But those who seek practical results in the present almost invariably enlist the past on their side. If it can be plausibly suggested that they have got the history wrong, and if they decline to consider the possibility that they have, they may end up looking as if they believe that any serviceable past will do. Their credibility is likely to suffer, not just as to opinions about the past but also as to aspirations for the future.

But there are larger questions yet – questions about the health of public debate in this country. A set of changes which, it seems fair to suggest, would hardly have been anticipated before the second half of the twentieth century has brought about an intensity of debate not known previously. Among these forces must be reckoned the emergence of the dark side of our colonial past from the obscurity of ignored protests into the open arena of public attention, the exploration of that dark side and its implications for the future, the affirmation of Maori identity and an aspiration to a distinct Maori political future, and a divided response from a sizeable body of Pakeha participants, some for and some against this new environment.

It is a situation fraught with danger as well as with hope; especially with danger if debate becomes a simple matter of one dogmatic assertion trying to stare down its opposite. Much of the debate is historical: how did we get here and what can we do about it? That is the point at which the Waitangi Tribunal exists. More than any other agency, it has prompted a new look at our past and a new look – hopeful for some and ominous for others – at our future. Maybe, with this central role, it should be more ready to get into discussions about what it is doing? At the very least, it would be valuable to the Tribunal itself if its work were carried out in the context of informed public opinion. There would be a more knowledgeable consideration of these matters if they were widely debated within the historical profession; Tribunal and Crown historians, with a wealth of experience, should be free to join in.

But there are wider reasons. I would like to see more attention devoted to a different history – one that took as its starting point the interaction between two societies occupying the same physical space. The shared past will continue to be disputed ground; that is unavoidable when lasting divisions are part of the historical inheritance. But that contestation needs, both for the well-being of the present and the integrity of the past, to be qualified by an acknowledgement that integration is also an unavoidable inheritance. Without that balance, there is danger in dwelling upon dividedness; with it, there is a chance that division will be an opportunity and a benefit.

Because the claims process is unavoidably adversarial, it will continue to identify – and probably to exaggerate – our inherited divisions. That tendency needs to be tempered by a historiography which emphasises integration at least as much as separation and conflict. While this more inclusive history would not conceal the harm integration has brought to one of the two peoples, it would not take that as the end of the story. It would go on to recognise that, for good as well as for ill, those peoples have been and will remain inextricably bound together. This recognition would help to mitigate, if no more, the tensions that typify our present and will surely last into our future.

CHAPTER TWELVE

A History to Live By

In the year 2000, a year I had anticipated in my childhood with a sense of wonderment, I experienced for the second time a radical shrinkage in my professional life. I remained an editorial consultant with the DNZB in its new and reduced dispensation, but the occasions for consultation have shrunk away to nothing. The *Dictionary*, all ten volumes in two languages, has been committed to the world wide web, whether for its well-being or not I remain unsure. The proud and bustling establishment that once filled a floor of a city office block with people, activity, ambition and achievement, and spilled over into libraries, archives and museums throughout the country, has shrunk to a 'residual' unit, now located in the History Group of the Ministry for Culture and Heritage.

Something of the dislocation which accompanied my formal retirement in 1990 has again occurred. I miss the foothold, the place to go to and come from high above Lambton Quay in between visits to the bank and the pharmacy. A place in which to pause and catch one's exponentially shorter breath, to have a word with this one and that one and to sustain the illusion that you are still part of the world of work. But, it is at least to be hoped, as the exterior horizon shrinks to the suburb and the street (but not yet and with luck not ever to the bowling green and the chat room), the interior horizon may be helped to expand.

To end my working life as an inactive consultant with an agency of state dedicated to heritage, history's shifty cousin, is not without its ironies. Whatever doubts I may entertain as to culture in this official context, I have always been wary of the notion of heritage. One might even argue, a little dourly, that history has nothing to do with heritage, that its business is not to celebrate the treasures of the past but to scrutinise inherited pieties and, if need be, to take them apart. That is a high ideal – and historians should always accept a duty to attack the misuse of history by politicians, propagandists and all manner of high priests. But the pursuit of heritage does not necessarily, or even normally, entail misuse; it is more a matter of pressing history into the service of transient and too often superficial social aspirations, and that is a problematic business. An unsatisfying impermanence broods over the treasures of the past when they are held up for our admiration; one generation's cherished achievements are likely to be effortlessly forgotten or vigorously discarded by the next. Who, today, would seek to celebrate the virtues of British settlement? Or be reminded, as I was as a child, of the glories of imperialism on Empire Day? The luckless fate of Waitangi Day must surely serve as a warning: the one-nation aspirations which underlay both the creation of a shrine to the Treaty in the 1930s and the effort to convert its anniversary into a national day in the 1970s have vanished in a puff of protest; it has become an emblem of disunity.

In raising a small alarm about an overzealous cultivation of heritage, I do not mean to undervalue state sponsorship of history – the rich benefits of which are evident in the long connection of the Department of Internal Affairs with historical research and publication, from the Centennial series of 1940 and the War History volumes to the output of the Historical Branch, still active as the History Group in its new location. Not least amongst these benefits can be numbered the government's several initiatives in reference publishing. History, these examples testify, may do well under the shadow of the state. And that shadow is no more than an unequivocal manifestation of a common condition – of the pressures which society exerts upon historians and scholars generally, not only on those who work directly for taxpayers' money. There is no pure scholarship, and it would be a dull life if there were; even the most sheltered scholars must concede that considerations other than the scholarly shape their work – research leave, promotion, a better job, the esteem of colleagues and a reputation in the world. To work in public history as the servant of the sponsor-state (as I have done for a number of years) is only to accept a more transparent version of the common professional condition.

Historians can hardly avoid playing a public part, nor can they be expected to keep out of politics. But they will do themselves and their discipline and, in the end, their cause (if they embrace one) a disservice if they fail to live and work in that tense but lively space between the imperatives of society and of scholarship – if they do not manage to temper the demands of commitment with those of truthfulness. Whatever the location in which historical work is done, it carries with it, as one of the primary imperatives of scholarship, the duty to be critical, especially of those contrived versions of the past which are devised to confer a dubious legitimacy upon a partisan agenda.

If there is any firm conclusion to be drawn from history it is, I think, that the quest for righteousness, whether or not pursued by historical means (and most are), is a hazardous business. All pieties, orthodoxies and programmes, including one's own, are open to question and should be treated with suspicion. The critical imperative I have tried to heed, and the cultural imperative I have tried to temper, together make up the kind of history I have – or so I hope – managed to live by. And, in practice, the two imperatives need not be far apart. A critical history which avoids both self-congratulation and self-condemnation, which is aware of the impermanence of programmes, icons and fashions, which encourages inclusiveness and contestation and which, in sum, is not too sure of itself, could have immense benefits for political discourse and dialogue.

Ours is a society in which histories abound, narratives through which people locate themselves in the present by evoking a past and staking out a future. Each particular history leads into a series of wider histories, of families, localities, associations, countries and, I suppose it is theoretically possible, the world. My own narrative, as I have tried to tell it in this book, has a good deal to do with families and localities and not much (apart from places of employment) with associations such as tribes, clubs and political parties. I have always found myself uneasy with the demands of close-knit social groups. Churches, with which I have had prolonged dealings, are no exception; most are not especially close-knit, and when I rashly entered one which sought to be I chafed at its sanctions well before I gave it up.

Nor does my history, personal and professional, have much to do with 'the world'. It has had everything to do with a country, the one I belong to, and with the few other countries with which my individual and cultural ancestry links me. Globalisation may be the future, but I cherish the hope that I will manage to avoid making it mine; those places and times to which my ancestry and affinities connect me provide a sufficient set of identities. The world and the multitudinous histories that constitute it do not much engage my attention. When I took up Fernandez-Armesto's *Millennium* I gave it up after only a couple of hundred pages, unable to see what most of these exotic empires and episodes had to do with me. A less indulgent judgement would note that the author's declared intention of cutting Europe down to size might have had something to do with my disinterest.

If it's a matter of histories, and if everybody needs one, it might be enough to say 'Here's mine' and leave it at that. A broadcast programme I once heard on oral history had someone declaring with great emphasis: 'If it's my story it's true and no one can tell me otherwise.' I do not have that kind of certainty. Even as I say 'Here's mine', I cannot avoid adding 'I hope I've got it right' and trusting that whoever tells me I have got it wrong will do so gently. For one of the central pillars and supports of my house of history – the other is doubt and scepticism – is a respect for evidence and for argument anchored in it, a respect which has managed to survive those demonstrations that evidence is no more than a mirror for the perceiving self. I know that I can be wrong, and that there are ways in which I can be shown to be wrong, about both my story of myself and the history I use to understand myself.

The decision to tell that story and to explain it to myself as well as to others is part of a shift of attention away from the enveloping world of restless activity towards an inner world of recollection and reflection. This shift has been occasioned, in part, by an intermittent feeling of being something of a stranger in the world into which I have survived. I am tempted to think that I have lived to see, not exactly the end of civilisation as we know it, but at least the beginning of the end of the settler New Zealand I once thought I knew. That sentiment is, of course, absurd; to entertain it is to teeter on the edge of generational self-indulgence. Settler New Zealand is still with us; the change is simply that it is no longer as hale and hearty as it – deceptively? – seemed to be when I began to explore it. Over the closing decades of the twentieth century the fissures of race, gender, class and generation have grown deeper and wider; that has required us to accommodate more in the way of unsettlement. The spirit of the times has changed and acquired a sharper clarity.

The 'times' I have lived through have been diverse, untidy and anything but homogeneous; they contained many alternatives and contradictions. The times have summoned some to enlist in war against the evil of their days and others to reject war and the notion that any war can be just. For some the times spoke of sexual freedom and for others of strict marital fidelity; for some the dismantling and for others the strengthening of the welfare state; for some accessible abortion and for others none at all. The list of interdependent opposites could go on and on; typically, I have found myself looking either way and never without a slight twinge of sympathy for both.

While this habitual hesitation did not stop me from enlisting on the side of this good cause and that, I have also found it difficult to hold an unambiguous opinion even when I wanted to. My inclination has always been to the left; more a matter of 'no friends on the right' than of 'no enemies on the left'. An upbringing that emphasised social responsibility and activity, an education that instilled liberal values, and a history curriculum that gave prominence to reformist movements (and, as well, to their unexpected outcomes – a prime source of scepticism) left me with little option but to be something of a socialist and something of a liberal.

The spirit of the times, if that is what these conditionings express, made it certain that I would be, successively, for Indonesian independence (almost reflexively), against peacetime conscription (in a vestigially pacifist manner), for the Communist victory in China (but more because it ended a mess than as a new start), for the watersiders in 1951 (with reservations), against the curtailment of civil liberties in the same year (without any), for nuclear disarmament (but with some respect for the balance of terror), against the death penalty (quite unambiguously), for a nuclear-free Pacific (while wondering if it mattered), for decolonisation (but, as time went on, with a clearer perception of its limitations), against the Korean and Vietnam wars (hesitantly in the case of the former), against apartheid and the Springbok tour (but glad not to be in New Zealand in 1981) and for the assertion of indigenous rights as against the beneficial inheritors of the settler state (while pondering my own ambivalence as one of the latter).

Some of my own age and of a leftish disposition will recognise in this chronicle of causes a pattern close to that of their own agitational lives. For others of my contemporaries it will be a list of the occasions upon which they either looked the other way or enlisted on the other side. For those who are younger it may appear, at best, a chronicle of old, unhappy, far-off things and, at worst, not even an echo of battles long ago. Perhaps I am closer to that response now than when I found it next to impossible not to make a stand, even if a quiet one in the background. It is a relief to discover that there are many matters upon which I do not feel the need to have an opinion. I find it hard to explain both the activist itch and its disappearance; age alone will not do. Perhaps it is a sense of the probable success of the worst option – bad money will always drive out good.

The same uneasy combination of an ingrained radicalism tempered by conservative caution has had its influence on all that I did in history, from the *Story of New Zealand* to the submissions to the Waitangi Tribunal. This ambivalence may well have brought about a lack of thrust, a regular recourse to 'on the other hand' and a paucity of firm findings. In teaching and research supervision I did not want to make converts or to shape opinions; for the most part I limited myself to asking what were the grounds for holding a particular opinion. As an editor I did not consider it to be my business to correct the opinions of contributors, unless they were patently implausible. This quality has, of course, its downside; my failure or inability to agree that there was an obvious right way played its part in bringing about domestic disharmony. While I can now wish that it had not been quite that way in family matters, I persist in thinking that it was a good way to teach, write and publish history.

This is an account of my professional and more or less public life; however, as the impact of endemic uncertainty upon both writing history and being a parent suggests, it would be improper wholly to avoid situations in which public and private intersect, or to ignore personal events of such magnitude that their omission would lead to distortion. The account of my origins, parentage and upbringing at the beginning of this book is a family history but, with my second family, I have done no more than name and place our children, who arrived with such reliability in three groups of two, in the early 1950s, the early 1960s and at the turn of that decade to the next: John Benedict and Steven Mark; William Hugh and Thomas David; Elizabeth Mary and Matthew George – names which reflect family connections, religious inclinations and a traditionalist approach to their giving. Between them they have (at present) five children, and I am constantly aware of the privilege it is to be a grandparent. Earlier I have said a little about my marriage to Dorothy Rachel Nielsen; it lasted, through some transformations, from 1951 to her death in 1988. Here I wish simply to emphasise her goodness, her devotion and her courage.

The scope of my present life – after a decade of sometimes strenuous freelancing, a continued involvement in public history, a persistent inability to leave a book unreviewed and, now and then, a tendency to get into ideological scraps – has both narrowed and deepened. I have been surprised to find myself attending more than before to that fugitive essence we might call the inner self and to its oneness with my sadly neglected, abused and resentful body, and so to those kinds of awareness and activity through which it may still be possible to move a little further down the path of self-realisation. Though it was not begun in that spirit, this book has come to occupy a place in that attempt, by way of looking down the track I have trodden with an eye to the shorter one that lies ahead.

The years in which this book has been written have also been the years during which my long friendship with Bridget Williams deepened into a personal commitment. This is a consequence as unanticipated as any of the redirections recounted here. It reminds me that all the goals one strives for, whether achieved or not, count for less than these boons – unconvenanted mercies, in an older language – which arrive as unexpectedly as they are unmerited.

In a surprising way, my dealings with religion, which have been noticed on quite a few of these pages, have passed through a rejection (with a sigh of relief and an unaccustomed sense of peace) of creeds and affirmations to a growing feeling that, while it is not helpful to think of something or somebody 'out there', I had better think more attentively about the likelihood that there is an 'in here' which I have neglected. This has gone along with a turning away from the more stringent side of the Christian tradition – the one which insists that we eradicate those things we are instructed to consider evil and sinful. It now seems clear to me that the effort to get rid of them in fact strengthens their hold, and that it is better to examine them and ask what they are trying to say. This I understand to be something of a Buddhist approach, not that I am in search of yet another denominational label.

People are apt to say that they would prefer to live in another time; and others that they would always opt for the one they have lived in. It is not an especially real question – no one can know another time in the way in which one knows one's own. Preferring another time is really a statement about the life one would like to have had but could not. I have once in a while hankered to be a canon in an eighteenth century English cathedral, not hampered by too much in the way of doctrine or duties and with the liberty to get on with a peaceful life of obscure scholarship. In another mood I have thought that I would have enjoyed being a gentleman publisher in England in the 1920s, the companion and patron of aspiring poets and novelists, with a secure corner for long lunches in a London pub. Dream on – but temper the dream with the sharper knowledge that in neither milieu would I have risen, given my antecedents and upbringing, to such pleasurable heights. If I give thanks for my own times, and I do, it is because they are times in which it has been possible for one with that background to enjoy some of the privileges and pleasures of scholarship and literature – perhaps, too, some of the responsibilities. These are my reasons for preferring my own time. Simply, twentieth century New Zealand was a good place for the son of an immigrant farm labourer.